THE SUNFISHES

THE
SUNFISHES

REVISED AND AUGMENTED EDITION

JACK ELLIS

Illustrated by David Taft

LYONS & BURFORD, PUBLISHERS

Published by special arrangement with Abenaki Publishers

Printed in the United States of America

Design by Laura Joyce Shaw

10 9 8 7 6 5 4 3 2 1

Library of Congress Cataloging-in-Publication Data

Ellis, Jack, 1936–
    The sunfishes / Jack Ellis ; illustrated by David Taft.—Rev. and augm. ed.
        p.   cm.
    Includes bibliographical references.
    ISBN 1-55821-356-2
    1. Sunfish fishing. 2. Sunfishes. I. Title.
SH691.S76E45   1994
799.1′758—dc20   94-23536
                                                    CIP

*This work is dedicated
to my brethren of the angle
who have yet to experience
the joys of warm water.*

CONTENTS

ACKNOWLEDGMENTS

When I accepted Bob Johnson's offer to write a book on warm-water fly fishing, I had no idea of how much fun it would be. It has indeed been a labor of love. When the going got a little rough, Bob and Jeff Hines were always there to help me out and provide encouragement. Without their support and expertise this project would never have begun, let alone concluded.

I want to thank Corey Rich, of Houston, who first published my "Reflections on the Pond" column, which led to this opportunity, and Jack Russell, of *American Angler* magazine, for my first national exposure. Excerpts from my column and previous articles in *American Angler* are scattered through this text. I owe a debt to Chuck and Sharon Tryon, of Rolla, Missouri, who first encouraged me to write about my fishing experiences.

I also owe a great debt to my dear friend and coworker, James Ewings, of Chester, Texas. James's knowledge of East Texas fish and wildlife is mindboggling and he willingly shared it all with me. Without the benefit of his many years of field experience on local waters I never could have learned to catch sunfishes, let alone write a book on the subject. He manifested the patience of Job, stoically listening for hours as I recited the text of this book and stopping to correct me when I "had it wrong." He tempers my "book learning" with an appropriate, and much needed, ration of pragmatism and common sense.

And speaking of stoicism, my dear wife, Darlene, provided invaluable assistance in insect collecting, fly tying, proofreading, and various clerical chores. I can't say she didn't complain, but she did endure my awakening her every morning before daylight so she could listen to the fruits of my night's work.

FOREWORD

Selective bream? Yes, indeed! The only question is, why did it take us fly fishers so long? Why wasn't this book written years ago? Maybe it's the relatively recent and rapid expansion of fly fishing. Maybe it's that most anglers are no longer satisfied with limiting their fishing to a couple of trips a year to trout country. Or maybe, it's just that we had to wait for the likes of Jack Ellis.

Reading Jack's manuscript brought back many childhood memories. Bluegills and kids just go together. These scrappy, eager fish taught me a great deal about fishing. Then, there were the early morning rides on the milk truck to a friend's farm where we stalked largemouth bass in the pre-sun fog, casting our popping bugs into the reeds and waiting tensely for the explosive take. And I can still feel the soft breezes of late evenings when the smallmouth of the Allegheny River and French Creek grabbed our minnow imitations with gusto. These were my teachers, along with the trout, and I have not forgotten them.

Jack points out that the fly fisher can readily adapt trout tactics to bream. And how true it is. Bream eat the same foods as trout, they can get selective and downright ornery in their feeding habits, they require the same flies and tackle as trout, and they live in wild, beautiful country. For the sometimes trout fisher, bream are the perfect fish. They keep our skills sharp, they keep us thinking, and they give us deep and lasting memories.

Similar problems require similar solutions. Thus, the fly fisher that solves a problem on a bream lake can often take the answer directly to a trout lake and immediately apply it with success. And vice versa. But bream fishing also has its own unique problems, and Jack has addressed these very knowledgeably. He has carefully and thoughtfully explored the world of the bream and given us this seminal book, pointing out those areas in which we understand the bream and those areas where our understandings are, as yet, weak.

Bream fishing offers the fly-fishing community a new and exciting area in which to explore fly designs and angling techniques. From this exploration will come a host of original ideas that we can translate into fishing for other species. This cross-pollination of ideas is evident in Jack's work, and it is the main strength of this book. *The Sunfishes* is recommended reading for anyone who presumes to the Waltonian title of "The Compleat Angler."

I'm glad to see that fly fishers are at last paying serious attention to this all-too-often-neglected fish, and I can think of no one better than Jack to carry the banner.

—Gary Borger

INTRODUCTION

Fly fishers have always considered themselves to be a cut above the rest of the fishing world, trends toward populism in recent decades notwithstanding. I daresay that Dame Juliana's vesper prayers included a plea for deference toward those good sisters who weekly cast a seine upon the convent stream to capture the evening meal. For centuries ours was a pastime of the privileged nobility, the clergy, and landed gentry, involving intellectual and artistic subtleties that eluded the common folk of the English countryside. We have inherited this aristocratic legacy, and genuine fly fishers still consist of a small, fastidious group of patricians drawn, for the most part, from the apex of the socioeconomic pyramid. I was once caught up in that era of feigned egalitarianism, determined to bring the joys of fly fishing to the masses, but, with the sagacity of advancing age, I have come to accept the futility of such endeavors. We march to a different drummer.

We are a discriminating lot, with very specific preferences, not only in our methods of angling, but where we fish, the species we seek, the milieu in which we practice our art, and in our choice of angling companions. My purpose in writing this book is to advance the premise, which I passionately believe to be true, that sunfishes, in certain types of waters, are as worthy of our future efforts as have been our beloved salmonoids for the last five centuries. But if I am going to sell this fishery to my angling brethren, I must be perfectly honest at the outset. Sunfish waters (and to an increasing extent, trout waters) that satisfy our needs for solitude and tranquility are found mostly on private land. This is especially true of the warm-water fisheries because of the proximity of large population centers to public lakes and rivers. It has never been fashionable to tout private waters in American angling circles, but the frontier is gone and quality angling, as we define "quality," will not be free and public in the coming century. This is the unvarnished truth, and pretenses to the contrary are counterproductive.

My introduction to the southern fishery was, however, on a public lake. I grew up, fly rod in hand, on the trout streams of the California Sierras but moved to the Gulf Coast during the oil boom of the 1970s. It seemed to my wife and me that our lives would henceforth be lived for a single two-week trip to the western mountains each summer. We encapsulated ourselves in an air-conditioned environment, complained about the humidity and mosquitoes, and dreamed of the high country. We were strangers in what seemed to be an alien, hostile land.

But that was before a certain Saturday morning twelve years ago that would forever change our lives. I had just finished a size 18 Quill Gordon, which I added to an overflowing box of unused trout flies. We had shut ourselves in the house for several consecutive weekends, unable to bear the steaming Houston summer, and I suggested that perhaps we ought to give this warm-water fishing a try. Darlene was absolutely horrified. "Have you lost your mind?" she shouted. "Go out into those insect-infested swamps to be bitten by a snake or eaten by an alligator! Unthinkable." After some spirited discussion, we bought a boat and motor that very afternoon, along with several cans of Off, a snake-bite kit, and a number of books on the flora and fauna of the southern ecosystem. That night we headed for the Neches River valley in East Texas where we camped in a ramshackle motel on the banks of a large, shallow lake.

The first gray light of dawn gave us a glimpse of this strange, new habitat. The entire lake seemed to be studded with moss-draped cypress trees. A dense layer of fog hung low and eerie over the dark water. A squirrel began chattering in the branches above us, awakened by the morning light. An armadillo, grotesque in his prehistoric armor, lumbered noisily through the underbrush. There was life all around us in this wet, sylvan environment.

As I clamped the motor on the little boat, Darlene tied a size 12 California Mosquito on a 5X tippet and roll cast to the nearest cypress stump. I heard a splash, followed by a squeal of delight. Her six-weight Fenwick sported an impressive bend; the line was slicing zigzags through the tea-colored water. Moments later we admired a handsome, saucer-sized bluegill complete with a big orange breast and a hump on his head. "West Yellowstone it ain't," she said, "but it's beautiful in its own way."

Our zeal for this fishing increased with each passing season. With increasing expertise, our respect and admiration for these fine game fish grew. Warm-water fly fishing had become an all-consuming passion by 1983 when we quit our jobs in Houston and moved to the Neches River valley where it had all begun. We now fish these waters daily from our new home deep in the pineywoods of East Texas.

Although a part of our hearts will always be in the Sierra Nevada, and we still dream of the evening caddis hatches on the Henry's Fork, we have discovered exciting new horizons of fly fishing. We don't feel that we have broken faith with the traditions of the five centuries since the good Dame cast her first fly on the convent creek. Rather, we feel we are building on that tradition, and it is my heartfelt prayer that He will give my pen the eloquence to encourage our brothers and sisters of the angle to join us in this wonderful world of warm-water fly fishing.

It is indeed scientifically inaccurate, and quite unfashionable these days, to attribute humanlike emotions and cognition to fish. Nonetheless, I am offended when angling authorities refer to our beloved trouts and sunfishes as unreasoning feeding machines with pea-sized brains that only react to stimuli. I apologize to the reader for my unscientific approach, but the heroes of this story are the intelligent residents of my home water who are quite capable of anger and terror; they love certain foods and hate others; they are happy when the water temperature is warm, miserable when it's cold. They recognize my crude attempts at imitation and possibly even laugh at them. When I lose a big bass, "he" got away. Hopefully, even the most ardent feminist of readers can accept my use of the masculine pronoun. That fish is my friend and my affection is too great to rudely refer to him/her as "it."

—*Jack Ellis*
Woodville, Texas
1991

1

THE SUNFISH CLAN

We hadn't gone very far that first morning on Texas water before we encountered a crusty old gentleman running a trotline. We tried not to show our consternation—this was illegal activity in our native California.

"Howdy," I said. My feigned accent did not fool anyone. "Whatcha baitin' 'em with?"

"Brim," he replied. He shut off the antique Sears Roebuck outboard motor and turned the dilapidated jon boat in our direction.

"Little bluegill, you mean." I forgot to use the accent; Darlene glared at me with that "you blew it" look of hers. The old gentleman was indeed taken aback by my Yankee impudence, but he set down the bait pail and gave me my first lesson in warm-water fishing.

"You ain't from around here, are ya?" I admitted that we were newcomers from California. "Let me tell ya, son, there's lotsa different kindsa brim." He went on to explain to these uninformed city folks that some "have bigger mouths than others, that some have orange breasts while others may have red or yellow, and that gill flaps may be long or short and tipped with red, white, or blue. He showed us the "sun perch" he was using for bait. They were nearly transparent. Friendlier now, he assured us that all bream would "bite them little flies."

"Will crappie bite them too?" I inquired.

"White perch, you mean?" I nodded sheepishly. "I doubt it. White perch ain't brim. Ya gotta buy some minners fer them."

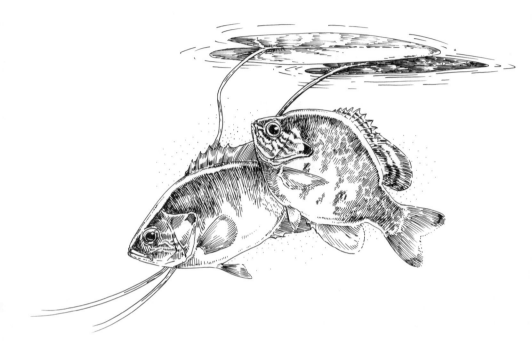

FAMILY CENTRARCHIDAE

That East Texas good ol' boy knew more about the taxonomy of warm-water fishes than I did. I could have recited the Latin name of every member of the trout family, but my ignorance of the sunfishes was nearly complete. I still find a great deal of misunderstanding, even among native Southerners, about sunfish and their place in the ichthyological scheme of things. Adding to the confusion is the use of the vague, nondescriptive, often offensive term of "panfish" among fly fishers. I am afraid that we are forever stuck with that unfortunate appellation for these fine game fish. Although I studiously avoid its use in my writings, editors invariably insist on putting it back in the text or title. It makes little sense to lump all these diverse species together under the "panfish" umbrella; the fish vary widely not only in size and appearance, but in dietary and habitat preferences. The term first appears in the literature in the early 1920s, two words then, as anglers discovered that these fishes did indeed have food value. I had hoped that the fish acquired the name because they resembled a frying pan, not because they belonged in one. I prefer to use the colloquial "bream," a corruption of the French *breme*, a type of European carp (*Abramis brama*). We probably owe the origin of that term to the early Cajun settlers in Louisiana. Even the misnomer "perch" is better than "panfish."

These are native American fishes that occur naturally nowhere else. They have always been our most popular game fish, owing in large part to their extensive distribution. They are more tolerant of disruptions in their habitat than are the trouts, and they are better equipped to cope with man's activities. Dams and reservoirs may be injurious to the cold-water fisheries, but they help the sunfishes. I once heard intelligence defined as "one's ability to adapt to changing environments." By that definition, sunfishes are certainly at the top of the class; they thrive in any oxygenated water that warms up during the summer, will eat virtually anything (even plant matter in a pinch), and can reproduce in sufficient numbers to survive any amount of predation. These aggressive, hard-fighting game fish will still be providing angling pleasure long after the trouts have succumbed to man's relentless onslaught against the natural world.

Only about a dozen of the thirty species in the family are of concern to fly fishers. Just as the Salmonidae group divides into several genera and subfamilies (chars, trouts, grayling, etc.), the Centrarchids (it just doesn't have the same ring, does it?) also conveniently fall into four categories of angling interest: (1) the basses (*Micropterus*); (2) the crappies (*Pomoxis*); (3) the rock bass (*Ambloplites*); (4) the bream (*Lepomis*)—the heroes of this story.

BLACK BASS

There are five distinct species of bass, along with a number of subspecies. I am familiar only with the three species found in East Texas waters: the largemouth (*M. salmoides*), spotted (*M. punctulatus*), and redeye (*M. coosae*) basses. That traditional northern favorite, the true smallmouth (*M. dolomieu*), does not occur in my Gulf Coast area. The spotted and redeye basses are quite similar to the true smallmouth, however, in both their preference for cooler, running water and in appearance. The fifth species, the little Guadalupe bass, is a native of the Texas Hill Country and does not range into the eastern part of the state.

I was distressed at a recent conclave when a fellow fly fisher drew odious comparisons between the largemouth and smallmouth basses. We have inherited an understandable bias toward insect-eating fish that inhabit running water. This is a completely arbitrary standard, and let's remember that any predatory fish whose diet includes organisms that we can duplicate at the vise is worthy of our efforts, regardless of the temperature, salinity, or clarity of his preferred habitat. The mighty largemouth is one of the world's great game fish, and he doesn't have to play second fiddle to his river-dwelling cousins.

I have heard of the northern smallmouth's superior fighting qualities for years. Ozark angler Ron Knight attributed that to the presence of current in smallmouth habitat. Ron's views make sense. The largemouth that I take from moving water do indeed fight harder and are generally more aggressive than those found in ponds and lakes. Although my own experience with *M. dolomieu* admittedly is limited, writers of an earlier era attributed any difference in the gameness of the two fishes, which Ray Bergman said was "very slight" at most, entirely to habitat. W. J. Loudon regularly caught completely wild specimens of both species from the same Lake Erie habitat nearly a century ago; he reported no discernible difference in fighting qualities. He added that current is the key variable. The Kentucky spotted bass is abundant in our tailwaters and creeks but the native redeye seems to be disappearing.

Big largemouth, those longer than eighteen inches or over three pounds in weight, require very different techniques and approaches than do the smaller fish. They tend to be nocturnal in ponds, deep in large lakes and, frankly, they don't interest me very much. Most of my fishing is done on ponds and creeks with regular trout tackle, small flies, and light tippets. I catch a lot of one- to two-pounders but normally lose the occasional lunker that grabs my bream fly. The conventional casting rod is an infinitely better tool for the trophy-oriented angler. Smaller bass, however, are regularly taken on the same tackle and flies used for bream and a two-pounder on my three-weight is all the fish I need!

WHITE AND BLACK CRAPPIE

"White perch" are second only to the largemouth in popularity. They thrive in large impoundments but tend to be smaller in pond habitat. Although this schooling fish lacks fighting qualities, he is delicious on the table. Crappies stay deep nearly all the time and rarely rise to a dry. The only trick to crappie fishing is locating them—once found they are easily caught on most any sinking streamer or mini-jig. They have, however, saved many a day for me when the bass and bluegills refused to cooperate.

The black crappie is more common in farm ponds and considerably more gamey. They will frequently take a topwater offering and seem more inclined than their larger cousins to feed on insects. Not as prolific as the white crappie, black crappies are less destructive of bass and bream populations and a far better choice for farm pond stocking. The black crappie prefers heavily vegetated areas, and I have taken two-pound individuals from a local pond that's entirely covered with lily pads. They are still quite gullible and easily caught, however—real dunces compared to the bream species.

BREAM

While crappies are the char of the sunfish world, bream are the trouts! Although limited in size, these intelligent insect-feeders are tailor-made for the fly fisher. They meet all the criteria of first-class game fish and are more than worthy of the serious angler's attention. There are eight species of bream that concern us. The bluegill is the star of the show, sharing center stage with the redear. The less common longear is similar to the bluegill in all respects, but the redbreast and pumpkinseed seem to prefer cooler waters; they are found only in creeks and tailwaters along the Gulf Coast where I fish. Although the green sunfish, warmouth, and rock bass will readily take a dry and feed on insects at least part of the time, they don't match the bluegill and other smallmouthed bream in either stamina or degree of angling challenge.

I advise warm-water enthusiasts to carry a copy of McClane's *Field Guide to Freshwater Fishes of North America* in a vest pocket. Identification is complicated by natural and introduced hybridization, but I am sure that most fly fishers want to know what they're catching. The illustrations and text in that comprehensive manual are adequate to permit identification in most cases.

Bluegills reach truly gargantuan proportions in our rich, tepid ponds and commonly weigh a pound. They have learned to survive in a very hostile environment. They demand the angler's best tying and presentation skills, as we shall see in subsequent chapters. I am talking about mature fish here, not the little sunfish that school in the shallows. Like all sunfish, the adult bluegill will recklessly attack anything that comes near his spawning nest, but as the season progresses and normal feeding patterns resume success requires all the skill and persistence the angler can muster. The redear is an equally desirable game fish—and his bottom-feeding habits make him even more challenging than the bluegill. Except during the spawn, the redear will test the mettle of even the most talented nymph fisher.

The green sunfish is extremely handsome in maturity and will take a dry or streamer with gusto. Unfortunately, like the crappie, he gives up quickly and lacks endurance. Green sunfish readily cross with bluegills and the resultant hybrids sometimes reach four pounds! The farm-pond angler will soon learn to recognize these widely stocked hybrids and discover that they retain the fighting nature of the bluegill. Warmouth and rock bass are often confused and are interchangeably called "goggle eye." In East Texas, rock bass seem to prefer the cooler water of inlet creeks and are not usually found in warm ponds. Warmouth are more common, even predominant, in some waters. All of these largemouthed sunfishes are prolific minnow feeders and considered undesirable by lake managers who will usually ask you to kill them. Don't throw them on the bank, though. They are a delight when served with a bottle of good white wine.

SURROGATE SALMONOIDS

We all share an image of the classical fly-fishing model—an angler alone on a pristine stream, surrounded by gorgeous scenery, casting to big, wild trout within a stone's throw of his rustic log cabin. This is the ultimate standard that fly fishers, at least those who are steeped in the traditions of the sport, apply to any fishery. The components of the model—uncrowded conditions, clear running water, scenic beauty, big trout (and all of that close to home)—are becoming increasingly elusive for most anglers. By necessity, we must make substitutions in the classical model; to decide how far and in what direction each of us can go with these compromises.

If the rest of the image is in place, we have learned to accept the presence of other anglers. We are willing to travel thousands of miles in quest of the otherwise perfect model. Some of us have compromised the current and accepted still water; others live without postcard scenery and will even fish in murky water. We are often forced to settle for smaller trout, and many of us can even rationalize the substitution of other species of fish—if they eat insects, live in attractive surroundings, and have a degree of stamina and intelligence.

There is one criterion, however, that is inviolate and beyond compromise. The one element that must be present for the art of fly fishing to be practiced in any sort of meaningful way, is embodied in the word *wild*. Without wild fish, our efforts constitute nothing more than an irrelevant exercise in futility—a vicarious sort of angling much like tying the leader to the cat's tail! Our sport requires wild fish, and if we have no access to them, we might as well put our rods in the closet and angle nostalgically in the pages of our rich fly-fishing literature.

I recently received a letter from a warm-water enthusiast who lives, of all places, in southern Maine. He sadly reported that all of the traditional cold-water resources in his area have been ruined by put-and-take stockings. He cannot accept such a fishery, and he and his friends now fish warm-water ponds where fish still feed, spawn, and complete their life cycles in a natural way. Such high latitudes are not friendly country for the Centrarchids, and the fish are probably small, but this discerning New Englander has made that painful substitution in the classical model. He has admirably refused to compromise the prime criterion of wildness. From his perspective, the south is still an angling paradise with thousands of square miles of freshwater lakes, literally millions of farm ponds, and countless miles of creeks and rivers—all of them teeming with truly wild fish.

Some of us can accept such surrogate species more easily than others. I number among my valued acquaintances a gentleman angler of singular intellect who passes many a dreary midnight pondering over ancient tomes of angling lore. He is an immutable sort of man who sadly demands that the classical model remain intact; the only compromise he has been able to accept is to occasionally cross continents and oceans in search of it. His fine cane rods gather dust and moths are slowly converting his laboriously tied collection of Catskill dries to a fine powder. When I visit him, he always pours two snifters of vintage French cognac, hands me a real Cuban cigar, and then we journey back to yesteryear—back to the wild trout and sparkling waters of his beloved Adirondacks and my High Sierras. Even as we journey nostalgically in the past, sharing precious memories of special moments in time, more temporal fish rise to tiny winged ants on a crystal pond nestled in a sylvan southern glade just a short walk from the ornately panelled study and plush leather charis where we sit.

Although he accepts on an intellectual level my arguments that the Centrarchids are worthy of the serious angler's attention, he nonetheless spurns my urgings that he give them a chance. He cannot overcome the more subjective and emotional aspects of his mind-set, and despite his failing health, which makes travel difficult, he will never cast a fly on warm water. We both share the same classical model of perfection in the mind's eye. But, for me, there is only one sacred, inviolable component—*wild*. For him there are two—*wild* and *trout*.

The Centrarchids are, of course, a salmonoid surrogate in the view of any lettered and sophisticated fly fisher. To claim otherwise would be to deny five centuries of tradition. They are, however, a worthy surrogate and, unlike the domesticated hatchery rainbows that profane many of our hallowed streams, they feed and spawn naturally. The prime criterion of wildness remains uncompromised. If the reader can appreciate these fine game fish objectively they will, in time, win his affection and one day occupy a place in his heart alongside our beloved trouts.

2

THE WATERS

Smaller waters are the fly fisher's natural element. While floating a farm pond on a summer evening, surrounded by rising fish, I experience the same solitude and the same euphoria that I remember feeling on the then uncrowded trout streams of my native High Sierras. There is no "high," natural or otherwise, to compare with a rise to your dry just as the last rays of light disappear over the western horizon. You walk back to the car in the dark as a new moon peeks through the pines and the wild sounds of the night surround you; you're wet, tired, and hungry, but blissfully happy and utterly content. The rewards of fly fishing cannot be measured in pounds of fish, miles traveled, or dollars spent on rods. None of that means anything if one is denied the solitude to commune with nature and her wild creatures. Farm ponds offer that very solitude, and I have never heard it more beautifully expressed than in a note I received from Dallas fly fisher Jeff Hines after a visit to our East Texas camp:

> . . . after admiring and releasing my final fish of the day, I paused before kicking back to shore to gaze at the full moon rising in the clear night air above the tall pines on the eastern shore of the pond . . . a vee of ducks glided silently upward, above the tree line, waving to me in the water below. I attempted a photograph of the scene reflected on the mirrored surface, trying to capture the moment on a small piece of celluloid. I hoped the fleeting rays of light would yield a faithful image of this pinpoint in time, but the reality is that no picture, no words, no imagination can replace it—you just have to be there.

9

Thousands of beautiful lakes and ponds, the vestiges of a former time when the family farm was a viable institution and old King Cotton ruled the southern landscape, lie nestled in the pine plantations and hardwood forests of the Deep South. Some of these charming little jewels are found on land that has been subdivided into weekend and retirement homes for affluent urbanites, but most of these ponds remain unfished and generally ignored by the cattle ranchers and timber companies that own them. Collectively, they comprise a resource of incalculable value to the growing ranks of warm-water fly fishers. Here we can practice our art in a quiet, tranquil setting without the distractions of screaming bass boats, floating beer cans, and tournament mentalities. Here our senses are assaulted only by the cries of quarrelsome crows and the drumming of the pileated woodpecker. Here, surrounded by the verdant beauty of the southern woods, we can cast a dry fly to unsuspecting, wild fish.

Although these ponds are located predominantly on private land, I believe most fly fishers can gain access to one with a little effort. Much timber company land is under lease to hunting clubs, and they have been amenable to granting access rights during the spring and summer.

Rural bankers, real estate brokers, and agri-business people are generally acquainted with pond owners and may arrange an introduction. Make inquiries among friends, neighbors, and business associates.

The landowner must be assured that, in granting access privileges, he is not opening a can of worms that will lead to problems. If he has had a bad experience, his lake may be off limits to everyone. In any case, he must be reassured that you will not bring guests to the lake nor share it with anyone else, that you will close gates so his animals don't escape, and that you will generally respect the property. A little knowledge of agriculture is helpful. Dairy cattle, for example, must not be disturbed or upset in any way or their production may decline, and a hog may ingest a big popping bug that has been carelessly left in a bush.

Bringing someone with you is anathema—at least until your relationship with the landowner is well-advanced. People tend to be paranoid about liability in these litigious times, and the landowner may be more comfortable just "looking the other way" rather than granting formal permission. Try to be sensitive about his concerns and to anticipate his objections (which most often remain unspoken). Children,

KEY:

1—*Plankton*
2—*Duck Weed*
3—*Water Hyacinth*
4—*Bushy Pond Weed*
5—*Cattails*
6—*Pond Weed*
7—*Coontail*
8—*Water Prim Rose*
9—*American Lotus*

Common Water Plants of the Gulf Coast

especially, make landowners very jittery. A nine-year-old boy drowned in a local farm pond a few years back. The owner was sued and nearly bankrupted—despite the fact that the father was the truly negligent party—because he had allowed the father and boy to go fishing. Also bear in mind that many rural folks still are inherently suspicious of well-educated "city slickers." In my early days in the rural South, before I understood the culture, I tried to lease a beautiful, fish-filled pond on a farm owned by a widow. I had my attorney draw up a contract and presented it to her. Although we took great pains to completely cover her exposure to any conceivable problem, she flatly rejected the agreement out-of-hand and leased the place at a fraction of my offer to a hunting club. I was dumbfounded. Did she really prefer high-powered rifles to a single fly rod? As my cultural sensitivity increased, I came to realize that she simply was frightened by my formal approach. The hunters spoke her country language; my big-city attorney did not. She said she didn't want "to get involved with a bunch of lawyers." I now handle such matters with a friendly visit over coffee.

This will take a little of what salesmen call "ice-breaking" work, but it's more than worth the effort. If you encounter a landowner who is rude or hostile, don't get discouraged. The next fellow may be a prince. Tell him you practice catch-and-release exclusively. If he expresses an interest in fly fishing, give him an outfit and teach him how to use it. If the lake needs stocking, open your wallet. If the dam needs repair, spend a weekend helping him. You get the idea. Most fly fishers are business and professional people who deal with such matters daily.

Other private waters are readily accessible on a fee basis. Champion International, for example, welcomes responsible anglers on their beautiful 800-acre impoundment near Lufkin, Texas. The company charges a nominal fee to cover expenses. Membership lakes are appearing in the south and, although somewhat expensive, offer superb fly fishing. Quality per diem lakes are in operation near Dallas, Houston, and other southern cities.

We are gratified that public agencies are finally beginning to realize that not all southern anglers want to race around a huge reservoir hunting "hawgs," and we Texans are very proud to have the first public, warm-water catch-and-release fishery in the nation (Purtis Creek Lake, near Athens, Texas). The lake is managed with a limited-entry reservation system and strictly enforced speed limits. At this writing, Hector Macedo of the Dallas Fly Fishers is celebrating a ten-pound bass he recently took on a fly in Purtis Creek. This concept has been received very well by Texas sportsmen and more such fisheries are being planned. The U.S. Forest Service operates a number of superb small lakes and ponds in the national forests of East Texas, and that agency is putting greater emphasis on warm-water angling in other southern forests as well. These waters are well managed with special regulations and motors are usually not permitted.

In addition to small lakes and ponds, warm-water creeks, vast swamp areas, tailwaters, and large reservoirs all beckon to the fly fisher.

FARM-POND BIOLOGY

Although we use the term "farm pond" to describe any small, private lake, by definition, a farm pond (or "stock tank" in Texas) is a man-made impoundment for agricultural purposes—watering animals and providing irrigation water. They may be as small as a half-acre or as large as twenty or more acres. I read somewhere that there are a half-million such ponds in Texas alone. They are frequently stocked with channel catfish that are fed commercial fish food. In addition, bass and bream may also be stocked in the pond. Bream benefit from catfish feeding in two ways. First, they usually manage to consume a little of the fish food themselves; second, the well-fed catfish deposit nitrogenous waste on the pond bottom where the food chain begins.

All species of bream are notorious multipliers, and without the intervention of man or unusually high natural predation their numbers will soon surpass the food supply in a small body of water. Although I have seen healthy fish populations in ponds that have been unfished and neglected for decades, normally one of two situations will develop in a few years: (1) natural predators fail to control the bream population, resulting in a few large bass and countless minuscule sunfish; or (2) the bass get a foothold at the outset and populate beyond the available forage. In the latter case, the pond will contain large numbers of small bass, often grotesque in appearance with large heads and stunted bodies. But the bluegills will likely be huge. This is the situation where the very largest bream are found; the few surviving bream will enjoy an abundance of smaller food forms that the bass cannot utilize, including certain parts of aquatic plants. Wading and diving birds, otters, and several species of rough fish also help to control bream. Although these predators are sometimes too efficient and may eradicate the entire population, landowners should remember that killing them may be illegal and probably is not in the long-term interest of the ecosystem. Channel cats will feed on small bream, providing the angler with delicious eating as a bonus, and specially designed traps are also effective in removing surplus sunfish. Lowering the level of the pond in the fall will deprive the juvenile sunfish of their protective cover and expose them to predation by bass, catfish, and other rough fish.

When I fish a pond for the first time I try to determine the status of the fish populations by using a variety of fishing techniques. Dozens of juvenile bluegills pecking at the hackles of a large dry fly tell me that the possibility of taking a lunker bass exists but probably little else. This pond would be a good candidate for night fishing with huge bugs. On the other hand, if a small streamer takes lots of small bass in the shallows, I know that big bream are undoubtedly prowling the deeper water and nymphs are called for. Sometimes, with the owner's cooperation, I use a seine net, wire fish trap, or even live bait to find out what's in the pond.

Stock tanks that are surrounded by hayfields or pasture are less scenic than woodland ponds but tend to be more fertile. These fields usually receive annual applications of high-nitrogen commercial fertil-

Fertility is optimum when you can barely see your hand when submerged to the elbow.

izer, part of which may leach into the pond. The chemical nitrogen, along with that naturally produced by grazing stock, creates a "bloom" of algae, which makes the water a putrid green and quite un-fishable. This condition may last for several weeks. If the bloom is too severe, the decaying algae will lower the dissolved oxygen below the fish's minimal requirements, resulting in a massive fish kill. If the bloom remains within tolerable limits, which it usually does, the algae die and fall to the bottom where they nourish a variety of small organisms. The nutrients travel up the food chain and, if natural predation and/or management prevents a population explosion, eventually produce those fat, feisty bluegills that we love to catch. Biologists even recommend creating such a bloom by adding chemical fertilizer to private lakes that have no other sources of nitrogen. The chemical is added slowly to maintain about eighteen inches of visibility (or when you can barely see your fingers with your arm submerged to the elbow). Extremely clear water is frequently a symptom of low fertility in warm-water habitats and not as desirable as in the trout stream. It may be aesthetically pleasing, but such a pond most likely is short of nutrients—and the fish will be small.

Accepting murky off-color water is a very difficult adjustment for a trout fisher. I had a hard time until I realized that crystal clarity is neither natural nor desirable in this habitat; it may also indicate that the pond is too acidic. Phytoplankton doesn't do well in water with a low pH and fish are also sensitive to acid. Serious bass fishermen carry pH-testing equipment in their boat and avoid acidic areas of a large lake. When pH falls below about 6.5, the pond should receive an application of agricultural lime. Acidity is a major problem in the southern pine belt, whereas alkalinity is a factor in many areas of the West.

Unintentional doses of nitrogen may cause massive growth of aquatic vegetation. The whole surface of a shallow pond may be choked with weeds. This is good sunfish habitat, and such a pond is probably full of giant bluegills. Don't pass it up if you can find any little hole to present the fly. While weeds are good for the fishing, many landowners feel the need to control them with selective herbicides. Chemical companies claim that these agents are harmless, but I still hate to see them used. The introduction of vegetarian grass carp (Asian white amur) often results in the elimination of all the weeds, which may ruin the pond. Nutria, an imported, plant-eating rodent, burrow into levees and cause washouts. The best control, in my opinion, is mechanical removal; build a plywood raft on two jon boats and simply rake out the weeds.

Large numbers of turtles can also be detrimental, but their impact is often exaggerated. They rarely overpopulate in woodland ponds (raccoons keep them in check) but do present problems in subdivision lakes. Turtles lay their eggs in nests that they dig on the bank, and coons, skunks, and snakes are quite adept at finding the nests—thereby maintaining an acceptable population. Homeowners generally discourage such critters, inadvertently causing an overabundance of turtles in their ponds. Turtles are best removed by trapping or with a .22, if you're a crack shot. Bear in mind, however, that some species are endangered and protected by law. Baby turtles are frequently taken by young, uneducated bass. They can be a factor in our fly tying, with certain limitations, as we shall see in Chapter Four.

While green water signifies fertility and "black" (tannin-stained) water is equally desirable, I avoid muddy water. Yet bass and other fishes can survive, even flourish, under very muddy conditions. The rivers of America's heartland have carried millions of tons of silt to the Gulf of Mexico since the last ice age, and many native fishes actually evolved in perpetually muddy water. I know that there are a lot of bass in the chocolate-colored Neches River, near my East Texas home; trot-

KEY:

1—*heron*
2—*snake with fish*
   in mouth
3—*plants*
4—*red-ear sunfish*
   eating a snail
5—*school of minnows*
6—*scud*
7—*bass eating*
   bluegill
8—*crawfish*
9—*dead algae*
   raining down

The Warm-water Food Chain

liners catch them all the time and a few are even taken on lures. I just can't bring myself to fish in such water, but that may well be a self-defeating attitude. We recently enjoyed a visit from Kansas anglers Ron and Sheryl Knight. They said that muddy water was the norm in their area; they fished it regularly with success. They use spinner blades and other large, noisy lures and advised us to do the same. As long as we have a little "pretty" water, however, I'll probably leave the Neches River to the catfish crowd.

The amount of suspended silt in a pond depends entirely upon the nature of the watershed. Undisturbed woods or perennial pasture will not create muddy conditions, but logging, construction, or certain farming operations can destroy a small lake. I have had permission to fish a beautiful fifteen-acre lake for a number of years. It was a great little fishery with lots of bass, bream, and white crappies. Unfortunately, the Texas Department of Corrections decided to build a prison unit on the feeder creek, and the subsequent clearing and construction have turned the lake into a mud hole. The fish are still there; we haven't seen any dead ones. They must be continuing their regular feeding and spawning routines, and the mud probably bothers us a lot

more than it bothers them. The landowner accepts the situation in the name of "progress" and encourages me to continue fishing, but the appalling brown water turns me off. One of these days I may be able to overcome my prejudices and give it a try. I may be surprised! In time, of course, the lake will settle out and may even be the better for it. Fly fishers considering the purchase or lease of such a property should look very closely at the watershed. Are there other lakes upstream to catch the silt? Who owns the upstream watershed and is it likely to be developed? Is the timber big enough to cut in the near future? Failure to consider such matters could result in a heartbreaking situation later.

Many lakes on private estates, recreational properties, or in subdivisions are managed for sport-fishing. If professionally managed, they may want you to fill out a catch log after each visit and kill certain species of fish. By all means, cooperate with their policies. Gar, bowfin, carp, and other rough fish should be killed along with small sunfish. I do believe, however, in releasing large bream. It takes several years to grow a nine-inch bluegill—a prime fly-rod game fish. I've never seen a pond overpopulated with big bream. Estate maintenance people commonly put alligators in these ponds to control beaver, nutria, and otters. If someone has been feeding them, they could be dangerous. Be sure to ask.

FARM-POND STRATEGY

Successful angling involves more than simply learning how best to take advantage of the feeding response of a fish. It also depends on an angler's ability to avoid the things that frighten fish. Anything that simulates a predator will put down fish—whether it's the flash of light off the guides or the shape of the fly line as it sweeps through the air.

Indeed, the very sight of the human form strikes terror in the hearts of all wild creatures—great or small—so the prudent angler takes care to stay out of the fish's window of vision. I know trout fishers who approach a trout stream with great stealth and finesse, but who throw caution to the wind in warm-water situations. They slosh into a farm pond like a grizzly bear and start flailing the water with forty feet of heavy line. Sunfishes face a much longer list of potential predators than do trout, and they are in peril constantly. Since they live in a more hostile predator-filled environment, warm-water fish—mature bluegills especially—are particularly attuned to any potential danger. Natural selection eliminates careless individuals early in life. Only the brightest and fittest ever reach maturity.

Yet, if the sunfishes were as timid as trout, they would soon starve. Sunfish must feed and spawn in the very shadow of imminent death. Danger waits behind every log and clump of weeds. Heron stalk the shallows; gar, bowfin, channel catfish, and loggerhead turtles lurk in the depths; fish hawks and kingfishers patrol the skies; and the deadly snake bird rests only momentarily between dives. The otter works the pond by day, and the cottonmouth and alligator work it by night. The sunfish that reaches adulthood has developed great skill in dodging his enemies and accepts frequent close encounters as a normal part of daily life. That's why stealth, finesse, and delicacy need to be part of every warm-water angler's vocabulary. You must take care not to mimic inadvertently the telltale sounds of a swimming otter or diving cormorant by noisy wading, sloppy casting, or indiscreet use of swim fins.

Bass and bream react quite differently to predators. Bass are much bolder because they occupy a higher place in the food chain. They do not subject the fly to such close examination, are rarely tippet shy, and are generally less spooky and more easily fooled than mature bluegills. The bluegill must expose himself in open water or shallow areas in order to feed, but the adult largemouth is an ambush hunter who lurks in the weeds, watching and waiting with malevolent intent. (Bass, as a matter of fact, are the leading predators of juvenile sunfish, as well as yearling bass, in most waters.) Bluegills usually forage in the safety of groups and dash toward deep water when the alarm is sounded. The bass is a loner who simply slides back into the cover and remains motionless until the danger has passed. Stealth and finesse are, therefore, much more important in the pursuit of bream than of bass. When bluegills are spooked, it's all over. But an alerted bass does not usually flee and will soon calm down; he usually decides that the hairy creature that landed noisily in front of his lair doesn't represent danger after all.

Big bream, on the other hand, require the same delicacy and finesse as wild brown trout. Bluegills will immediately leave the shallows when they hear a commotion on the pond, and even under the best conditions 7X tippets and tiny nymphs are often required to induce a take. Boats, float tubes, paddles, and swim fins cause combinations of sounds that effectively imitate otters and diving birds; mature bluegills simply will not tolerate that, especially in the clear water of mid-summer and fall. They will head for the depths and remain there until the activity ceases—in other words, until the angler gets out of the pond! A float tube must be moved very slowly and quietly with long, motionless pauses. Watch the behavior of the cormorant; you will see that it never stops moving—it is constantly swimming, diving, landing, or taking off. We often unwittingly imitate that deadliest of farm-pond predators with sloppy casting, noisy pick-ups, noisily kicking the fins, and even by dragging weeds behind the fly. Bass are also alarmed by those sounds, but they tend to react with caution rather than panic.

Sunfish seem to learn which disturbances represent danger and which are safe. They are even attracted by certain noises. They may feed near swimmers or adjacent to heavily traveled powerboat lanes, but clam up and hide when they hear an electric trolling motor, an electronic signal from a depth sounder, or the whirling blade on a spinnerbait. These intelligent fishes can even distinguish between an animal and an angler. I have seen spooky bream actively feeding around the legs of wading cattle, only to panic and head for deep water when my human form entered their window of vision. I have considered dressing in a cow suit, but I'm afraid the bull might mistake me for one of his harem. Now, that's a sobering thought! Seriously, domestic bulls can be dangerously aggressive, and you should never enter a cattle pasture without conferring with the rancher first. I once failed to do so, and spent two hours swimming in a pond while a 2,000-pound Hereford bull snorted and pawed menacingly on the bank. He finally left and I dashed for the fence. I returned the next morning, this time in the rancher's pickup, to retrieve my new rod. The huge bovine, who carried a classy pedigree and was worth over $20,000, had stomped it to shreds.

Every farm-pond angler has seen the wakes of fish moving out of the shallows when he brazenly approaches the pond. It is actually quite difficult to approach a pasture pond without spooking fish out of the shallows; most likely, you'll see fish moving toward deeper water while you are still some distance away. Just sit down for a few minutes. They don't stay frightened for long and will soon return. Time spent silently watching and waiting is not wasted because relaxed observation will reveal much to the studious angler. He may detect subtle movements of reeds or cattails or may even see the fish themselves as they cruise the bank. Many northern fly fishers believe that we southern anglers never see our prey and only cast blindly to likely habitat. On the contrary, much of our farm pond fishing involves sight casting to visibly feeding, spawning, cruising, or basking bass and bream.

While we all prefer the comfort of a float tube to crawling around in thorny brush and mud, it may be a luxury that we cannot afford. The very act of launching the tube usually frightens the whole aquatic community, at least for a few minutes. Bank fishing is often the only way to effectively present a dry fly to big, non-spawning bluegills. They are much more difficult and challenging than bass, and you should be very proud of every fish over nine inches that you take on a dry—and you will take more with a stealthy approach. I can state unequivocally that such fish will not remain in the shallows when you are sloshing around in a float tube. The tubing angler, with his noisy kicking and splashy casting, is continually alerting them and maintaining a perpetual state of alarm. I used to fish with a fellow who always took his two children and their cocker spaniel to the pond. The yelping dog would jump out of the car and run around the edge of the pond at top speed. The screaming children would always be in hot pursuit. The fish tore out of the shallows so fast they made roostertail wakes. Yet the fish returned within minutes once he got the exuberant youngsters under control. The tuber should discipline himself to move slowly, and occasionally he should sit quietly for a few minutes to let the pond settle down.

Some years ago, I heard one of America's most respected trout fishers state in a lecture that warm-water fish did not require as much delicacy and finesse as cold-water species. Such assertions are misleading: the two fisheries cannot be accurately compared in that direct manner. Yes, some sunfish, such as the white crappie, are gullible, but so are some salmonoids. In fact, brook trout are pretty dumb! The adult bluegill is in a class by himself. He, not the black bass, is the real star of the warm-water show. But this challenging little game fish is the Rodney Dangerfield of the fly-fishing world; he has never gotten the respect he deserves. There are several reasons for this. His aggressive spawning behavior masks the discernment, caution, and intelligence that he shows the rest of the year; anglers have failed to distinguish between juvenile and adult fish (the young of all species are easy to catch); and, finally, his prolific abundance in diverse habitats has somehow made him less desirable. Dave Whitlock, our leading authority on warm-water fly fishing, has discovered that mature bluegills are more challenging than four-pound browns! In an historic article in *Fly Fisherman* (May 1991, p. 58), Dave tells it like it really is, eliciting a chorus of cheers from southern fly fishers:

"... try sight casting to a one- or two-pound bluegill in a clear spring pond with a two-weight rod, thirteen-foot 7X leader, and size 18 scuds. I did recently and had a *harder* [emphasis mine] time with these small permits than any four-pound rainbow or brown. I sight cast to eighteen or twenty bluegills, spooked all but six . . . and landed two pug-faced fish in the pound-plus class."

We southern anglers have always been stepchildren in the fly-fishing community, and we are understandably gratified that our fishery is finally receiving national recognition. One crusty Texas fly fisher (who happens to own one of the best private lakes around) finished the article and commented that "they ought to run Whitlock for President." While I'm quite certain that Dave's ambitions don't extend that far, he is a hero among Texas fly fishers!

All sunfishes are very structure-oriented. They have certain preferences for water depths at various times of the year, and like all cold-blooded animals are very sensitive to temperature changes. It is, therefore, imperative that the angler familiarize himself with the bottom contours of a lake, the location of creek channels, submerged springs, fallen timber, deep weedbeds, etc. Begin by talking with the pond owner, who can probably give you the basic facts as far as depths are concerned. Then read about the behavior and habitat preferences of the black bass. Your knowledge of trout behavior won't help much here—you are dealing with a very different sort of critter. Some of 3M's bass fishing videotapes are helpful, especially "Understanding Big Bass" with Doug Hannon. *The Guide to Successful Bass Fishing*, by Rick Taylor, is a scientifically accurate textbook on the subject of bass behavior. Although these works are not fly-fishing oriented, they still provide the information we need. The habitat preferences and behavior of largemouth bass are covered in detail in the bass-fishing literature. I have included some of the better works in the bibliography. Also, seek out members of your fly-fishing club who have warm-water expertise and go fishing with them.

Southern waters are cluttered with weeds, brush, and dead trees. Fly fishing from the shores of a brushy woodland pond appears impossible, but with patience and the right casting techniques you'll be able to approach bass and mature bream without alerting them. The western trout fisher is not accustomed to worrying about his back cast or dealing with constant snags, and he may initially suffer anger and frustration. The eastern angler is more used to such obstacles and will adapt more easily. The best advice I can give is to keep your cool; don't get mad and start cursing the trees! You're out there to enjoy yourself and to commune with nature. The number of fish you catch is irrelevant. You will lose a lot of flies; if you don't already tie, you soon will.

The dirt road that leads to one of my favorite ponds runs along the inlet creek channel, about 100 feet up the embankment from the creek itself. I used to drive along this road all the way to the pond's edge. I always saw dozens of large wakes heading down the creek to the safety of deeper water. As an experienced trout fisher, I realized that bass and big bluegills were spending a lot of time up that creek channel enjoying both the cooler water temperature and the constant rain of summertime terrestrials tumbling out of the deciduous woods upstream. Now I park far away, sneak down to the creek, and am usually able to sight cast an appropriate terrestrial to a good fish. My caution is often rewarded with a breath-taking rise. With sufficient stealth and concealment I can usually get close enough to these fish to use a bow-and-arrow cast or a roll cast from the brushy bank. Any attempt to wade the creek will create total panic and pandemonium among its finny residents. In short, apply established trout-fishing techniques to the warm-water habitat.

KEY: 1—*pool below spillway*   7—*submerged timber*
      2—*creek channel*   8—*lily pads*
      3—*bass holding area*   9—*cattails*
      4—*submerged spring*   10—*bass spawning area*
      5—*overhanging hardwoods* 11—*pier*

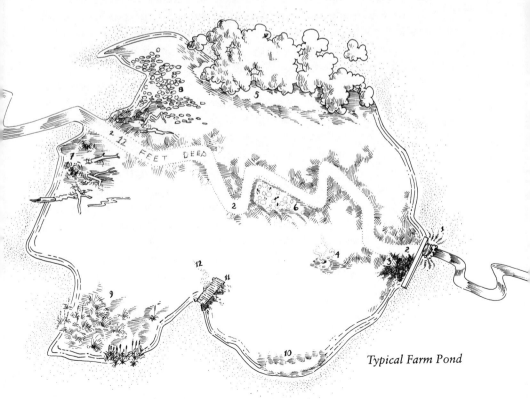

Typical Farm Pond

One hook-up will, of course, spook all the fish in the creek for a time. I then return to the pickup, which is parked well away from the creek channel, get my float tube, and walk down the road to the nearest access point on the pond. If I move slowly and quietly, I'll see fish moving back up the creek channel.

Upon reaching the pond, I sit quietly for a few minutes to get the feel of things and let the little ecosystem settle down. Are there any rises on the pond? What terrestrials are in the air? Is there movement of reeds or other activity in the shallows that betray the presence of spawning activity? Are squirrels active in the trees? (I have found that when other wildlife is feeding, the fish likely are too.) I may then take a surreptitious stroll around the lake, staying well back from the shoreline. My bellwether is the behavior of turtles; if the sliders stay on their logs, I know that the tranquility of the pond is undisturbed, but if they slide into the water, the alarm has been sounded. I look for cruising bluegills along the levee and bass in the shallows. I examine spider webs to see what has been hatching, and I look for recent damage to the foliage of pond side hardwoods, which indicates the presence of worms and caterpillars. I may also gain information for future use. Moth eggs on the underside of an oak leaf, a winged carpenter ant, or a single Hexagenia dun are all harbingers of hatches yet to come.

Only after I've acquired my data do I slip into the pond. This act will spook the whole community, so I sit quietly in the float tube until I see the turtles climbing back up on their sunning spots. The "all-clear" has been sounded, and it's time to start fishing.

The worst mistake is fishing too fast. We pick up the cast too fast; we retrieve too fast; we move along the shoreline too fast. I know from experience that even a little action in a given area means that fish are there, and my best strategy on a slow day is to remain at that location. Unfortunately, few of us have the self-discipline to do this even though we know that running all over the lake or spending the day driving from pond to pond won't do anything except vent our frustrations. When the fish feed in one place, they feed everywhere else as well. I have confirmed this by comparing notes with other anglers. Invariably, if I experience a period of good fishing at a certain time of day on a farm pond, anglers on a large lake many miles away report good fishing at the same time! There is no question that some external stimulus is triggering feeding behavior simultaneously over a wide area. Bass and bluegills seem to be much more affected by subtle changes in atmospheric pressure, weather, and possibly lunar and solar factors than are trout. They tend to feed in binges and then remain inactive for a matter of hours or even for several days. Although it seems to smack of medieval astrology, there just may be something to these feeding charts. Sometimes feeding periods are explainable in terms of weather and water temperature; I know, for example, that any sort of easterly wind will kill the fishing. But, just as often, the fish turn on and off for no reason. At this writing, for example, the pond in front of my house has been covered with rises every afternoon between 2 and 3 PM. Terrestrial insects and other wildlife have also been active in mid-afternoon, lending credence to the solunar theory.

It has been my experience that trout can be counted on to feed at some point during the day, but sunfish feeding seems to be something of a feast or famine situation. The secret is to be there when the feast occurs. I know an angler who bases his decision to go fishing on the behavior of the goldfish in his aquarium. He says that when the aquarium fish feed with gusto, the bass and bream do, too. If, on the other hand, the goldfish behave lethargically, he stays home. I believe him; it is absolutely consistent with my own observations.

The single-most significant factor is water temperature. I never paid much attention to this in my trout-fishing days—the water was always cold—but here it's crucial. I confess that I never carried a thermometer in my vest until very recently. I knew it was a good idea, but I preferred to use my hand. The water was either cold, hot, or "just right." My friend, Jeff Hines, gave me a thermometer, along with a book listing the temperature preferences of various sunfishes. He insisted that I avail myself of the data. As a result, my springtime and autumn angling has improved.

Since cold-blooded creatures lack the ability to regulate their body temperature metabolically, they naturally seek the most comfortable environment. This subject is covered at length in the bass-fishing literature, but certain fundamentals are worth mention here. Most of our angling is on or near the surface, and it is the temperature of that zone that most concerns us. In the cooler months of spring and fall, we find the best topwater fishing late in the day when surface temperatures are warmest. In the heat of mid-summer, dry fly fishing will be restricted to night and early-morning hours on the open pond; however, the dry fly may still be effective in shaded areas, creek channels, near submerged springs, or during rainy or overcast summer days—wherever or whenever the water is cooler. If the whole pond is uniformly hot, as it often is during the dog days of summer, the fish generally will settle down in the deepest water and remain quite inactive until the weather moderates. If an extended period of rain and overcast skies breaks the heat wave, all hell breaks loose for the dry-fly enthusiast. When those conditions prevail, take off work and go fishing!

Obviously, any sort of shade will probably harbor fish during the summer. The water beneath overhanging trees and bushes, piers or other manmade structures, lily pads or any sort of weedbed should be thoroughly fished during warm weather. One hot summer day, while I was float-tubing a familiar pond near the little town of Chester, Texas, my feet suddenly felt quite cold. I kicked on a ways, and they warmed back up. I turned around, went back across the spot, and again experienced the sensation of cold. As a later conversation with the landowner confirmed, I had discovered a submerged spring. I have since taken several nice bass from that spring on hot summer days. Some tackle shops in the south sell plastic "trees" that are designed to be placed in a lake for artificial shade. Boorish? Yes. But such devices have saved many a day for local bass guides on the large impoundments.

Although small school bass and white crappies will venture into open water to chase baitfish, bream will rarely stray very far from some sort of vegetation or cover. In fact, these fish appear to become disoriented when deprived of structure. If you place several bluegills in a uniformly colored tub or tank, they will mill around aimlessly, but when a small stick is placed in the tub, they will gather around the stick. I believe the fish are imprinted to orient to some sort of cover. In gravel pits and other sterile ponds, they orient to the bottom, along the shoreline, and even to a single pebble or blade of grass. Any sort of cover will satisfy their needs; a rocky, northern habitat is as good as a weed-choked pond in Dixie.

One type of structure that you definitely want to fish is a catfish-rearing pen. In recent years, state extension services have been schooling rural families on more efficient ways to raise catfish, and these "pens" are now a common sight on farm ponds. Normally about four feet square, constructed of PVC pipe and nylon mesh, the pen is designed to float and in the spring is stocked with about 250 catfish. The little fish are fed commercial fish pellets throughout the year and are harvested at twelve inches or so in October or November. The object is to keep the bream from eating the expensive fish food and to prevent bass from feeding on the baby catfish. Crafty little fellows that they are, however, bream hang around the pen to get any morsel of food that may escape through the nylon mesh. Not very idyllic, you say? Perhaps not, but I'll buy the beer if you can pass one without casting to it! Chuck Tryon, of Missouri, tells us that there is a deer-hair pattern to imitate the pellets (*Figuring Out Flies*, p. 62). Incidentally, it has been my experience that wild bass will not eat commercial fish pellets. (They won't eat anything that's dead, either.) Wild trout and bream will adapt to commercial feed, but even though aquaculturists have recently learned how to train newborn bass to eat pellets in a sterile environment, wild bass will starve to death rather than eat pellets. I believe that the refusal of a bass to stoop to that level is very much to his credit as a game fish.

Charlie Selover was a crusty old split-cane purist who had grown up on the pristine waters of upstate New York in the 1920s. He believed that a fledgling fly fisher should learn to observe and study the trout before touching the fly rod, and he demanded that I pass many days on the stream "fishing" without a rod before my first casting or tying lesson. Only now, nearly four decades later, can I really appreciate how his tutelage formed the basis for a lifetime of angling pleasures. He forced me to slow down and experience a feeling of oneness with nature and her creatures, to meld into the rhythm of the living stream in an unobtrusive way. Charlie didn't lecture on *how* to catch trout; he preached sermons on *why* we catch trout. Fly fishing for Charlie was spiritually edifying, and the number of trout in his old wicker creel mattered not at all. Delighting in the magnificence of the Creation was the only reward he sought. Although I lost contact with him many years ago, and I know that he is with his Maker now, I can still hear his admonitions to "dally a bit" whenever I am tempted to flail the surface of the pond and terrorize its inhabitants.

Angling with a fly is supposed to be a quiet, contemplative pastime. When the fly fisher approaches the water with frantic intensity, he is not only going to spook the fish, but he is also depriving himself of the deep emotional rewards that the experience should provide. Today's fly fisher doesn't live a relaxed rural life in an eighteenth-century farm house on the banks of the Battenkill. He can't stroll down to the river to calmly fish the Baetidae hatch after supper. More likely, he practices a profession in a concrete jungle, and his angling is restricted to occasional, hectic escapes to faraway destinations or tying trout flies that he will never use. If he also sojourns in the pages of our rich fly-fishing literature, he will realize that to cross the continent at the speed of sound to spend four unfulfilling days on someone else's water is to go through the motions without reaping the spiritual and emotional benefits of our chosen avocation. Productive cold waters may be inaccessible on a regular basis—he can't spend all summer on a farm in the Poconos—but the odds are that wild sunfishes are going about the business of survival in warm waters very near his home. If he visits them often, even in the city park down the street, he will participate harmoniously in their daily rhythm of life. Only then will he discover that satisfying contentment that is the essence of fly fishing.

THE WARM-WATER CREEK

The one memory of my youth in the Sierra Nevada that haunts me has nothing to do with the beauty of the trout and his habitat or his intelligence or selectivity. The sunfishes have all that in abundance. It's the sound and feel of running water. There is something about a moving stream that has a very special place deep in the soul of every true brother of the angle. Fortunately, there are still a few fishable creeks in the piney woods of my adopted Texas.

While all farm ponds are manmade, these creeks are natural. The creatures that inhabit them are absolutely wild. What the fish lack in

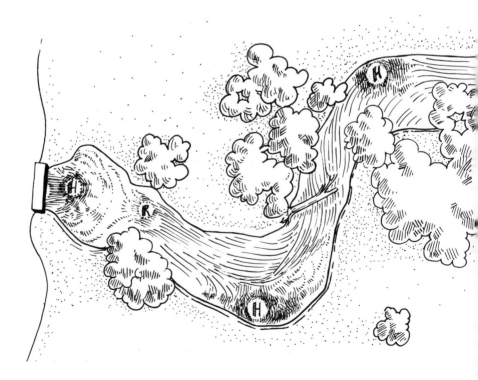

size they make up for in ferocity. The competition for each bit of food is so intense that bluegills cannot afford the time to study a fly the way they do in a fertile pond; they must savagely attack any offering or lose it to another fish.

Tackle and techniques are essentially the same as those required on a small, brushy trout stream. I normally overload my rod by two or three line weights so I can cast a very short line in the heavy cover normally present. Much casting will be done from a kneeling or crouching position to keep the line under the hardwood canopy, and conditions will often necessitate special techniques—bow-and-arrow cast, roll cast, steeple cast, and plain old "doodle-dabbing." Keep the leader as short as water clarity, which rarely exceeds two feet, permits. Southern creeks are rarely fished, and I can almost guarantee that you'll have complete solitude on any of them. Most people have better sense!

Creek fishing is not for the faint at heart, and sissies need not apply. It is, admittedly, tough habitat: it's snake infested; dangerous wasp's nests are everywhere; leeches will suck the blood from your legs; deep holes and alternating slick and soft bottoms make wading dangerous business; chiggers, ticks, and other terrestrial parasites, some of them vectors of se-

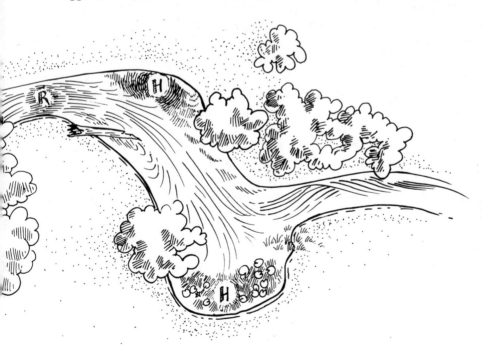

Creek-dwelling sunfish hold in the deeper holes (H) between sandbar riffles (R).

rious diseases, will cover your body for days if you fail to use repellent; and exposed body parts will be slashed by all sorts of thorns, many of them allergenic. Oh, did I mention the poison ivy, oak, and sumac plants that thrive in creek bottoms? Of all these discomforts, however, the wasps are the worst. I have been attacked by an entire hive, which required medical attention and an irate lecture from my doctor on the cumulative effects of Hymenoptera venom. I now take great care not to disturb a nest. If I see flying wasps, I throw sticks into the thicket ahead so I have some time to flee when they come swarming out of the hive. I have been hung up in thorns while trying to escape and suffered the wasp stings and the stickers together at the same time—all while dripping wet in 100 degrees of heat and 98 percent humidity.

I always run in panic when attacked by wasps, without regard for the safety of my rod or my person, but my friend, Fred Bunch, is a considerably cooler character. Fred, the photo editor for the *Houston Chronicle*, had accompanied me to the creek on a photo assignment when he disturbed a nest inadvertently while waist deep in the water. Fred is afflicted with male pattern baldness, but he restricted his reaction to soft cursing as the horrible Hymenoptera mercilessly and repeatedly stung his bare pate. In complete control of his emotions even as he suffered the agonies of the damned, he deliberately waded to shore, removed his expensive photography equipment piece by piece and carefully set it on a stump. Only then did his cursing become audible as he bravely drove the fearsome insects away with his bare hands. I have never seen such self-control. As we walked back to camp, I expressed my admiration. He shrugged his shoulders and confided that the Nikon he carried belonged to his wife, Betty, and that the stings were preferable to dunking it in the creek. After a stiff drink, he went right back to work. Now they tell us that "killer bees" are on their way from Mexico. I can't wait. I have sworn never to return to the creek after such terrible experiences, but the call of hungry, wild fish is just too strong.

These creeks are often loaded with small bass and bream, including the beautiful redbreast sunfish and rock bass. Many southern creeks are spring-fed and stay comparatively cool all summer. Heat-sensitive spotted and redeye bass inhabit these waters and are frequently taken on small streamers, nymphs, and dry flies. Most East Texas and Louisiana creeks consist of a series of deep holes separated by sandbar riffles. Floods have scoured the bottom to slick clay that is quite wadeable, but cleats are recommended. Waders are too hot and will tear on the omnipresent thorns and brush. Tuck your pants into your socks to discourage leeches.

Siltation, the result of logging operations, has taken a heavy toll on the native mayflies that were once abundant in southern creeks. Except for a few Odonata nymphs and possibly some caddis larvae, bottom samples will reveal a paucity of aquatic insects. Dipteran hatches, including Chironomid midges, are daily occurrences but these fish depend heavily on terrestrials, and the angler's attention should be on the complex insect community in the deciduous canopy. The best time to fish these streams is during the late summer when the water is low and arboreal worms and caterpillars are most abundant. You may even observe a hatch of spent, female acorn weevils. (Try to find that one in the pattern books!) If willows line the bank, lacewings and ladybugs can be expected. These predatory insects lay eggs in colonies of willow aphids and bream are commonly observed taking the spent females as they drift downstream. Hatches of giant craneflies and dispersal flights of various ants provide some very rewarding dry-fly fishing at times.

The trout fisher will be right at home on the warm-water creek—at least when he gets used to the hazards and discomforts and finds a source for gallon jugs of insect repellent and Calamine lotion. I highly recommend these creeks for the ecologically oriented angler or the amateur naturalist who accepts nature in all of her manifestations. Interestingly, I know one local fly fisher who always takes his wife to the creek. She doesn't fish, but she is an avid naturalist and loves the creek bottom. Give it a try. You may love it, too!

THE CYPRESS SWAMP

Few places in the Creation are more fecund than the temperate swamp. Whether his interests are zoological or botanical, the amateur naturalist will not be disappointed in this ecosystem. Life is everywhere in this dank, dripping maze of twisting channels and narrow bayous. The atmosphere is often darkly forbidding, even evil, setting a melancholy mood reminiscent of Edgar Allen Poe's morbid lines, "Here through an alley titanic of cypress I roamed with my soul. . . ." One feels that he has travelled a million years into the past; you expect a dinosaur to stick his head through the foliage at any moment. Although a dynamic and ever-changing ecosystem, there is a certain timeless, eternal beauty in the depths of the swamp.

As one ventures deeper into this dimly lit world of grotesquely gnarled cypress roots and tea-colored water, the air becomes heavy with the smell of decaying vegetation. A strange silence prevails. Sun-

KEY:

1—cypress tree trunk
2—two-ft. wide band of open water
3—dense, floating coontail moss

top view

KEY:

1—Spanish moss
2—gnarled and twisted roots
3—coontail moss
4—cypress knees
5—largemouth bass
6—white crappie

side view

Swamp-dwelling sunfish hold close to cypress trees.

fishes, birds, and other friendly creatures become conspicuous by their absence. This is the realm of that most sinister of all freshwater fishes—the ferocious bowfin.

This prehistoric throwback is equipped with a special air bladder that enables it to survive in low-oxygen areas that cannot sustain other species. Also called grinnel, cypress trout, or mud fish, these aggressive predators eat any kind of living prey, including game fish, and may attain a weight of twenty pounds in the south. Areas of East Texas and Louisiana are literally infested with them, owing in large part to the fact that they are not considered edible by most people. We are hoping that recent increases in alligator populations may provide some natural control—if the bowfin doesn't eat them first! Despite his unsavory reputation, however, this trashy fellow has all the criteria of a first-class game fish. His dorsal is intermittently visible while feeding, providing the angler with a visible target. He is remarkably intelligent and discerning, often refusing the fly after close examination, and he fights as hard as anything that swims in fresh water.

Leave the trout gear at home—this tackle-buster demands the heaviest rod in your collection. He has a mouth full of razor sharp teeth capable of inflicting serious lacerations to the hand of a careless angler. A wire shock tippet is a must. He lives amongst the cypress roots, and no part of the leader should be less than twenty-pound-test. Casting is nearly impossible in the dense woods, so the angler must sneak up close to the feeding fish and present the fly right in front of him. It's sometimes quite difficult to induce a take, but when he engulfs your offering, hold on to your hat! Flies that ride low in the surface film, such as a Hare Water Pup, work better than noisy poppers. Sparsely tied Dahlbergs are also a good choice, but figure one fly per hook-up—the bowfin will cut it to shreds. I have taken them up to about six pounds. The larger ones I have hooked were utterly uncontrollable; landing them would have required, I believe, a very heavy conventional rod and reel in order to horse them out of the thick cover.

Several species of gar also reside in southern swamps and some anglers fish for them. Frankly, I can't get them to take a fly—they invariably pass at the offering and turn away. I must admit, however, that I haven't really worked very hard at it. Neither have I tried the poly rope technique. Supposedly, you simply tie a piece of white poly rope to the leader. There's no hook; the gar gets the rope tangled in his teeth. Everyone talks about this, but I have yet to meet anyone who claims to have actually caught one that way.

The swamp, like the pond and creek, is fly-fishing country. One is rarely bothered by high-speed bass boats, especially in the backwaters. Most of the angling pressure comes from trotliners, cane-pole bait fishermen, and old-style plug casters. These people are friendlier, more courteous, and generally less hostile to fly fishers than the tournament crowd. The latter make their fishing a deadly serious business, while the swamp fishermen, like us, seem to be out to have a good time, enjoy nature, and maybe catch a few crappies for supper. It is fairly common (and gratifying) to see someone casting bass bugs with an old Shakespeare rod, automatic reel, and a level line. I feel right at home in the swamp. One note of caution: the angler should not venture into backwater areas without local knowledge. It's very easy to get lost, and sudden releases from downstream dams can leave you "high and dry," necessitating an overnight stay with the mosquitoes and prowling gators. Proceed very carefully until you learn your way around.

PUBLIC RESERVOIRS

Most fly fishers avoid large public lakes. I think our negative attitude stems not from any intrinsic characteristic of the waters themselves, but rather from the ceaseless disturbance of high-powered motor boats. On weekends these places often sound more like the Indianapolis 500 than a place to go fishing, relax, and enjoy nature. The quiet milieu that we seek is further eroded by the organization of "megabucks" fishing competition, such as the outrageous McDonald's Big Bass Classic, which puts over 3,000 boats on Texas's Lake Sam Rayburn on a single Saturday. Bass fishermen love these affairs; they seem to have a "more the merrier" attitude. Sometimes I actually envy the fun they are having while I sit home sulking with jealousy of the big bass they are catching. We must remember that for every one of us there's probably a thousand of them; but, for that matter, the same situation prevails on many cold-water lakes and rivers where spinning rods commonly outnumber fly rods.

There are, however, some silver linings in these dark clouds. Fishermen spend hundreds of millions annually in the small communities that surround these lakes, and the black bass is well represented in the halls of state government. Our Texas lakes are very well managed, catch and release is widely practiced, size and bag limits are strictly enforced, and the fishing is excellent in most. I live in rural Texas and in recent years I have seen a dramatic change in attitude among hard-core bass fishermen regarding conservation. Organized fishing promotes catch and release, their leadership strongly advocates it, and releasing bass is now the norm. A dedicated bass-fishing acquaintance of mine is no longer on speaking terms with his brother since the latter killed and ate an eight-pound bass! Recently I witnessed a heated exchange in the local coffee shop—not over who had caught the most bass, but over who had released the most. These changing attitudes bode well for the future and along with larger minimum size and lower bag limits account for the heavy fish populations that we are currently enjoying in these lakes.

Although we find formal fishing competition repugnant, we must confess to a bit of hypocrisy. We conduct casting and fly-tying competitions and even fly-fishing tournaments in some places. Not a one of us can honestly say that we don't feel a little competitive with a fishing companion on the lake or stream. Competition is a natural part of human existence, and though I will never understand why someone who faces the rat race of life all week would want to carry it to the lake on the weekend it is not harmful to the resource when catch and release is practiced. Hopefully, the tournament people will find some way to release fish on the spot rather than carrying them around in the live well all day and releasing them miles from where they were caught. Even so, the fish do have a very high survival rate, and we see few dead bass around weigh-in areas. I am optimistic that someday big money prizes will be eliminated and replaced by trophies and some sort of honor system. Speaking of hypocrisy, a bass fisherman recently pointed out that many of us southern fly fishers also have power boats with big motors. "How come," he asked, "it's okay for y'all to run around the lake, but our boats are too noisy?" He suggested that we learn to tune out outboard motor noise. Not bad advice.

Indeed, big lakes, whether natural or manmade, whether in Texas or Alaska, have traditionally been avoided by fly fishers. They require a power boat, fish tend to be deep, and they always host a variety of competing recreational activities. Nonetheless, there is some superb fly fishing on these waters. I have caught more, and larger, fish there than on any of my farm ponds, but I still allow my own snobbery and sour attitude to deprive me of some great fishing. For years I've heard Dave Whitlock pleading with us to take advantage of these fisheries without being intimidated by the hardware casters. I intend to overcome these self-defeating prejudices and hope my warm-water brethren will also heed Dave's sound advice. I do admit that tranquility is elusive in such

KEY:

1—bass holding area   6—bass holding area
2—willows   7—inlet creek
3—bass spawning area   8—bass fisher
4—bass spawning area   9—fly fisher wading
5—lily pad field

Typical Cove on Southern Reservoir

places. Indeed, a boat roaring at fifty miles per hour into the cove you are fishing, coming to an abrupt halt as the wake rolls toward you like a tidal wave, is not conducive to the ambiance we seek. The situation certainly doesn't improve when the occupants set down their cans of Bud Light and start chunking spinnerbaits into the cover you are fishing, all the while making disparaging remarks about the "idiot in the inner tube." While you will occasionally experience such unfortunate incidents on public waters, the vast majority of bass fishermen are gentlemen and sportsmen and many are actually interested in fly fishing. Don't be surprised if boats just stop and watch you cast; taking a nice bass in front of such an audience is gratifying to say the least!

The secret to successfully fly fishing these reservoirs is to learn how to, in the words of one Texas fly fisher, "barricade yourself from Bubba." Most southern reservoirs have vast fields of lily pads, secondary shorelines of willows and brush that often conceal large flats and shallow areas, hundreds of acres of dense coontail moss or hydrilla, and impenetrable jungles of recently flooded brush and timber. The fly fisher should use these natural barriers to insulate himself from the hardware slingers and their noisy boats. Few bass fishermen will suffer the indignity of raising the big motor and attempting to maneuver the heavy boat by hand or with a pole into such places. By and large, these anglers won't go any place where they cannot use their electric trolling motors, and most will restrict their fishing to the edges of the cover. Most of their lures, except for the plastic worm, have exposed hooks that will hang up if cast into brush or lily pads. Moreover, their short stiff rods are a distinct liability. The extra leverage provided by the longer rod, if it's heavy enough to do the job, helps uplift bass out of heavy cover, and our weedguard-equipped flies are fishable in anything except fine, clinging moss. The superb habitat behind the weeds and cover is, therefore, largely unfished.

The typical bass fisherman has a love affair with his elaborate boat and wouldn't be caught dead fishing from a tube or other personal watercraft. Vive la difference! A warm-water fly fisher needs a power boat to transport his equipment to desirable areas, but as we shall see in Chapter 6 he doesn't have to fish from it to take advantage of the exciting wild fisheries in the backwaters of large impoundments.

All warm-water impoundments also have substantial populations of big bluegills. They are overlooked by most anglers and considered a pest by serious bass men. I have seen bream over two pounds taken on plastic worms from Lake Sam Rayburn in East Texas. They are most accessible while spawning, and the trick is to locate the bedding areas. Bluegills return to the same beds every year; once you have located them, you will find the big bream there every spring. The Corps of Engineers will generally lower the water level dramatically during a dry summer to satisfy downstream water demands, exposing large areas of lake bottom. This is the time to scout the shoreline looking for concentrations of the bowl-like indentations that betray a spawning area. The nests are also visible in clear, shallow water. Having located the bed, return the following spring when the water temperature reaches the mid-seventies for some really unforgettable fly fishing. This is somewhat more complicated than pond fishing. Not only is there a vast amount of water to face, but big bluegills sometimes will spawn in deeper water in big lakes. They move in from twenty or more feet to perhaps six to eight feet of water and spawn at that depth. A sink-tip may be required to reach them. However, if the beds have been located in advance, such presentation problems are easily solved.

During the summer and fall, mature bluegills will remain quite deep and rarely rise to a dry fly or bug. They frequent weedy areas, however, and high spots surrounded by deeper water will often host large schools of them. Bass fishermen generally know where they are since the big bream will hit their plastic worms—sometimes even taking the huge hook. An experienced worm caster can easily tell the difference between bass and bream strikes, and he will generally avoid those areas where the latter occur. He will, however, happily tell you where he was pestered by "bream bumps." Don't be bashful about joining in the bull sessions at the launching ramp! Upon arriving in the general locale you will still have some searching to do, however, since the fish will probably be scattered in little pods over a wide area. The sensible way to find the concentrations of bluegills is to pick up the casting rod and drag a worm through the area until you feel the bumps. I rationalize this by telling myself that I'm not really fishing with a soft plastic lure, but only using it as a searching device. Once the fish are located, anchor the boat or put out a small buoy (don't forget to pick it up later), put the casting rod away, and work out the fly-fishing problems. Determine the depth, choose the right line and leader combination, and try different patterns. You know the fish are there; now it's a matter of presentation. Finding fish in big, deep water requires flexibility in tackle selection. Take some bearings so you can return to the same place again.

The following principles will provide beginning guidance for the fly fisher who is considering the big-lake option as well as for the angler who is presently fishing them without success:

- Read the bass literature. There is much to choose from (see Bibliography).
- Concentrate on *one* lake and learn it thoroughly.
- Keep a detailed log book, being especially careful to note the exact location on the lake for each entry. This will require a little basic knowledge of coastwise navigation (piloting).
- Make friends of local bass experts and pick their brains.
- Buy a properly equipped boat (see Chapter 6).
- Adjust to the presence of other anglers and "tune out" the outboard motor noise.
- Fish on weekdays if possible.
- Don't hesitate to use casting or spinning tackle to find fish.
- When an area of fish is located, stay with it—even if they quit biting for awhile. Don't run aimlessly all over the lake.
- Carry your tube in the boat. Tie the boat to a tree and fish from the tube, or even wade, when conditions permit.
- Try to finagle an invitation to fish with a knowledgeable bass man. Use the casting rod while in his boat and don't pontificate about the virtues of fly fishing. Just watch him and learn.
- Acquire an accurate map of the lake and study it thoroughly.
- Take a Power Squadron or Coast Guard Auxiliary course in simple navigation. Learn to triangulate bearings, run a course and time, and interpret sounding data so you can return to the same spot or position yourself on a chart. Remember to consider the dramatic seasonal fluctuations in the depth of freshwater reservoirs.
- A large body of water is less intimidating if you concentrate on one small area at a time. Narrow your focus to one cove or a single square mile of flats and master that before moving on.
- Strive to overcome the negative attitude that we have (including yours truly) toward big water. There's a lot of fine fishing there for us. We are foolish if we don't take advantage of it.
- Acquire a full-sinking, sink-tip, and intermediate line and familiarize yourself with their use.

HOME WATER

It seems that jet-setting has become part of the fly-fishing world in recent years. The anglers of my High Sierra childhood all had a favorite
creek or stretch of river that they fished regularly. Some of the more
worldly and affluent went to the Rockies on vacation, but no one felt
the need to sail the seven seas in search of the ultimate angling experience. Some still manage to avoid the bite of the wanderlust bug. Bob
Marriott once asked Dave Whitlock why he didn't travel more and
take advantage of his many opportunities to fish the premier waters of
the world. Dave answered that he was too busy fishing the farm ponds
and trout streams near his Arkansas home. In so responding, Dave was
confirming a fundamental concept of angling—the importance of home
water to every serious fly fisher.

The temperature and salinity of one's home water is determined by
geographical realities and is less important than its accessibility on a
daily, or at least weekly, basis. Ours is a quiet, contemplative pastime,
requiring many relaxed hours of unhurried observation, collection, and
study. The angler develops an intimate relationship with the inhabitants of his home water and becomes familiar with their life processes
in all seasons and conditions. This relationship is the very essence of
the fly-fishing experience and it demands constant nurture, reinforce-
ment, and interaction.

We all enjoy occasional visits to a famous river or saltwater flat but,
as Emerson might have put it, such sojourns are for the angler's idle
time. The real business of fly fishing is conducted on one's own water,
which when fished regularly provides deeper emotional and spiritual
rewards, greater relaxation and solitude, and a more meaningful edu-
cational experience than hectic escapes to highly publicized destinations. Moreover, these costly trips are subject to the nuances of
weather, indifferent guides, and, worst of all, unrealistic expectations
which all too often lead to disappointment. (It always seems to be an
"off week" when I go.)

We Southerners are blessed with an abundance of homeless waters
begging to be adopted by some lonely fly fisher. There is a fishable
lake, farm pond, creek, or river within comfortable weekend range of
nearly everyone. In addition to the big public impoundments, there are
tens of thousands of private lakes and ponds all across the South, and
access may be as simple as getting permission from a friend, neighbor,
or business associate, or as affordable as buying an inexpensive lot in a

carefully selected subdivision. I strongly urge the warm-water enthusiast to seriously consider acquiring a weekend camp on a lake, pond, or river that fits his budget and his style. Any family will find incalculable rewards from such a retreat, as Doug Baker so eloquently expresses in his wonderful little book, *River Place.* Such properties are widely available in the South, often at bargain prices. An added bonus of such an acquisition is the likelihood that local associations will lead to invitations to fish additional private waters.

I think most lettered fly fishers would agree that nearly every angling great, from Walton to Whitlock, has made his most important contribution on his own home water. Each body of water is unique and success requires frequent and regular visits to the same place. Occasional outings here and there will most likely result only in discouragement. Choose the water that fits into your life, fish it regularly, and you will soon become a skillful and contented fly fisher.

3

BREAM ON THE DRY

An experienced trout fisher, even one who has never cast a fly on warm water or read a single word on the subject, would instantly adjust to a southern pond or creek. He may suffer some discomfort from the heat, humidity, and chiggers, but as far as the fishing is concerned, his knowledge, tackle, and fly boxes would serve him as well here as on the cold streams of the western mountains or a tree-lined spring creek in Pennsylvania. He has been trained to read the water, observe the insect life present, approach his prey quietly, and meld with nature. He understands the fundamental fly-fishing principles of study, observation, collection, imitation, and presentation, and he would have no difficulty in applying them to the warm-water habitat. With increasing knowledge of the ecosystem, he would modify the contents of his fly boxes to better represent larger southern food forms, but he would find little need for heavy rods and huge bugs. He would buy a mesh vest, to accommodate the climate, but the contents of its pockets would change little. He would find the fallen timber and brushy conditions not unlike many of the trout waters he had fished. He would not be deterred by the soft, cluttered, unwadeable bottom. He is no stranger to the float tube. He would find these fisheries more alike than different; in short, he would fit right in.

He would also recognize that many southern anglers are mired in the pre-Theodore Gordon nineteenth century as far as fly tying and basic approaches are concerned. They are still tying nondescript, rubber-legged attractors and seem to be oblivious to the myriad food forms in the ecosystem. They haven't learned that some understanding of the life cycles of insects will enhance the intellectual rewards of the fly-fishing experience immeasurably. Many anglers believe that warm-water fly fishing is a crude affair, involving nine-weight tackle and fist-sized bugs; they are apparently obsessed with big bass, ignoring all the other fine game fish in the lake. I believe the rewards that we derive from our fishing are directly proportional to the level of sophistication that we apply to it. Little wonder that warm-water angling has not received the respect that it deserves from the fly-fishing community at large.

The southern ecosystem is richer in both flora and fauna than is its northern counterpart, and warm-water fishes enjoy a much longer menu than do trout. Insects are only a part of the food chain, as we shall see in subsequent chapters, but their imitation represents one of the most enjoyable aspects of the sport. Although nearly all of the twenty-eight orders of insects are present in southern North America, there are six orders of primary concern to us—three terrestrial and three aquatic. The trout fisher will be familiar with all of the aquatics and most of the terrestrials that he will encounter in the South.

Of the "big three"—caddisflies, stoneflies, and mayflies—only the latter have real significance in our fishery. Incredible hatches of big Hexagenia emerge from well-oxygenated mud-bottom lakes, but due to the infrequency and unpredictability of these emergences, we are primarily concerned with the nymphal forms. Mayflies have a special place in the heart of every fly fisher, but they are less relevant in our fishery than are the Dipterans (mosquitoes, midges, and craneflies) and the Odonatans (dragonflies and damselflies).

Terrestrials are even more important in warm water. An incredibly complex community of organisms thrives in the deciduous forest and lush vegetation that surrounds southern creeks and ponds. In addition to the "terrestrial trio"—Lepidoptera (moths and butterflies), Hymenoptera (bees, ants, and wasps), and Orthoptera (grasshoppers, crickets, etc.)—a creek-dwelling sunfish may see winged termites, acorn weevils, lace-wings, carrion beetles, cicada, and a thousand other species as the seasons change. There are enough untied patterns in the southern ecosystem to occupy several more generations of creative tiers.

PRIMARY AND SECONDARY HATCHES

Nutrient-rich warm-water ponds are normally surrounded by lush veg-

etation and provide a laboratory-perfect environment for insect repro-
duction. Countless millions of "bugs" of every kind complete their life
cycles in and around these fecund waters, but despite frequent and
massive aquatic and terrestrial hatches, we don't always match the insect present. We often skip a link in the food chain and seek instead to
imitate the minnow, shad, or fry that is feeding on the insects.

Whenever large quantities of food are present on the pond, thousands of baitfish and juvenile sunfish are drawn from the shallows and
protective cover to feed on the "primary" hatch. These small fish comprise the "secondary" hatch, which the knowledgeable fly fisher may
prefer to address with an appropriate pattern. Understanding this concept is the key, not only to successful bass fishing, but to larger bream
as well. All species of bream, with the probable exception of the redear,
become minnow feeders in maturity. The warmouth, green sunfish, and
rock bass will feed primarily on small fish if they are available. During
hatches, small bass will charge repeatedly into the insect-feeding baitfish, often making quite a spectacle of themselves, but the big bream
stay well below the surface fracas and rarely show themselves. I do not
yet fully comprehend this behavior (limited water visibility precludes
observation), but I do know that during a midge hatch, for example, a
small dry will take mostly juvenile bream whereas a small streamer or
diver will take small bass. Bigger bass seem too lethargic to get involved in such nonsense. If I add a little weight to the streamer, I may
take a big bluegill. Much research remains to be done, but I expect
these preliminary observations to be confirmed. Without doubt, big
bluegills are the most difficult fish to catch in the warm-water ecosys-

tem; and they just might be the most challenging fly-rod prey of all freshwater fishes. To be quite frank, the only time I really take large numbers of big bluegills is during their brief spawning period. The rest of the year, each fish is the result of hard work and patience—even though I know the pond has a large population of big bluegills and that live bait fished deep will readily take them. Laugh if you must, but come fishing with me some summer afternoon and be prepared for a slice of humble pie at happy hour!

SELECTIVITY, OPPORTUNISM, AND DISCERNMENT

Fly fishers have traditionally admired selective feeding behavior and the fly-tying and presentation challenges that it implies. Fish that tend to feed opportunistically have generally been considered easier to catch and consequently held in lower esteem. There is, however, another variable in this equation—the *discernment* factor. The fish's ability to discern between real food and an imitation is, I submit, more indicative of intelligence than a tendency to zero in on a specific food form while ignoring other protein-rich naturals that come floating down the stream. In my amateur observations of the animal kingdom, I see no correlation whatsoever between selective feeding and intelligence. On the contrary, it seems that such behavior is most common among invertebrates and other lower life forms. More highly evolved organisms, including man himself, feed with aggressive opportunism. The fact that sunfishes are able to shift gears from moment to moment, in order to take advantage of the food available, is evidence of their greater reasoning powers; it is very much a plus from the angler's point of view. Their enthusiasm is, however, tempered by discernment. Every trout fisher has experienced the classic dry-fly refusal; a big brown comes out from the undercut bank, moves toward the drifting offering while the angler holds his breath, but turns away at the last second. Such refusals are constantly experienced by the serious bream fisher, and are worsened by the bluegill's habit of hovering under a dry for several seconds (which seem like an eternity) while he decides if this is something to eat. Any unnatural appearance or movement of the fly not only results in refusal, but most likely will spook the fish for the rest of the day. I have seen small trout take bits of debris during a hatch, but I have never seen a bluegill make that kind of error. He doesn't eat anything without checking it out first. This is one smart little game fish! Such "discerning opportunism" is yet another manifestation of the wisdom of Mother Nature; it is precisely the right behavior in view of the wide range of food forms in the warm-water ecosystem. The bass, in my experience, is much less discerning than his smaller cousins and generally easier to fool—probably because his ambush hunting tactic does not permit the luxury of close examination. Interestingly, bowfin, gar, and other warm-water rough fish seem to have evolved these discerning instincts to a very high degree, and it is difficult to induce them to take the fly. I am certainly not an ichthyologist, but it appears to me that some of these species use their sense of smell and taste to a greater extent than do the sunfishes. That puts us at a great disadvantage!

Bluegills will feed, however, quite selectively when two conditions prevail: (1) there is a lot of surface food present; and (2) surface water temperature is either very hot or very cold. The fish will briefly rise into that zone of discomfort to take the insect present, but generally ignores any other natural or artificial offering. I find it necessary to "match the hatch" during the dispersal flights of male fire ants in February and during the evening mosquito hatch after a sizzling summer day. I learned this lesson the hard way in my early days of warm-water fishing. I had invested in all the right "panfish" flies, mostly an assortment of various small poppers with names like Sneaky Pete and Dixie Devil. Darlene didn't go to such efforts and stayed with the same patterns she had always used on the trout streams of our native California. She was outfishing me consistently on the evening rise with standard dry flies, especially her California Mosquito. Obviously, the fish were feeding selectively.

My most dramatic lesson in selective bluegills came on one of those gorgeous late-winter days some fifteen years ago. I was not optimistic about the fly-fishing opportunities in Texas when I arrived during the oil boom of the 1970s. But after a winter of tying trout flies for my annual two-week pilgrimage to the western mountains, I just had to limber my casting arm somewhere. A nearby pond beckoned. Equipped with a little store-bought attractor with rubber legs and a gauche-sounding name, I decided to take advantage of the beautiful weather. Although the temperature was in the balmy eighties, the water was so cold that it hurt my hand. An hour of casting produced nothing, so I sat down in the pleasant sunshine, closed my eyes, and dreamed of Montana. I was awakened by the unmistakable slurping sounds of feeding fish—the surface of the pond was covered with rises! I jumped to my feet and began casting, but the little yellow popper was ignored. Closer examination revealed thousands of tiny winged ants. I ran to the house, pulse racing, grabbed a box of trout flies, and presented one of Darlene's tiny Black Ants to the still-rising fish. After I released a dozen of these handsome, orange-breasted bream, the feeding activity ended as abruptly as it had begun. The surface was still covered with ants, but the fish had braved the cold water long enough and had returned to the depths. That night I didn't pine for the Madison as I labored over my vise, for my heart was filled with the passions of a new love. Such experiences led to the conclusions above. Under normal conditions, however, a bluegill won't turn down a big juicy hopper— but for that matter, neither will a brown trout!

The bluegills on my home water will rise to fire ants and sometimes early-season Baetis mayflies in cold water, but they ignore the hatches of craneflies and certain midges that emerge when the surface temperature is in the mid-fifties. The reason, I think, is that the Dipteran hatches seem to occur in the earlier, colder part of the day, whereas the Baetidae emerge in the late afternoon when the surface is slightly warmer. Still, that doesn't explain why I commonly see unmolested Dipterans floating on the pond in the afternoon; perhaps their numbers are too small to stimulate surface feeding. Ant dispersal flights always occur, of course, during the warmest part of the afternoon.

Bream stay active through the winter, but their metabolism is so slow that they tend to be vulnerable only to a live bait, fished deep, when the water is below about sixty degrees. The temperature tolerance of sunfish species will vary geographically. Studies show that northern largemouth have a lower optimum temperature than southern fish. I would assume the same is true of bream. Textbooks state that bluegills start to spawn at sixty-nine degrees, but the fish in 'my ponds show no interest in sex until the water temperature reaches well into the seventies. Smaller fish have wider tolerances for temperature extremes than larger individuals. I commonly see both juvenile bream and bass in the cold shallows, but I never see big ones. Smaller fish can also tolerate very hot water because the size of their gills is larger in relation to their body (compared to larger fish), which facilitates their ability to absorb oxygen. This explains why I often take only small bass on my hair bug while the bass fisher is catching summertime lunkers on his plastic worm!

THE DIPTERANS

Although often viewed with mixed emotions, the evening mosquito hatch on a southern pond is pure heaven. Dozens of rising fish at twilight are a delight to behold and a joy to fish with light tackle and tiny dries. Since the surface temperature is quite warm after a hot, sunny day and there is usually a lot of larvae in the water, we can expect feeding to be selective. A regular dry fly is normally the most productive offering during the evening rise. Sometimes, however, only smaller fish will take the dry, and it may be necessary to sink a large larval pattern to get at the quality fish. I will use as large a dry as I can get away with, often presenting a size 12 fly to fish feeding on size 16 naturals, since the old "big bait, big fish" rule holds true in warm water. But if I go too far and present, say, a size 8 Irresistible to the larvae feeders, it is often ignored. Although the surface of the pond, where the mosquitoes are emerging, may be ninety degrees, it may be twenty degrees cooler just three or four feet deep. When the bream leaves that comfortable zone and rises up into the hot water, he has, I think, a mosquito on his mind, and he simply doesn't have time to examine other food forms that may be present on the surface. If, however, an item of food slowly sinks down into the cooler water, his normal discerning opportunism will be functioning—and he has time to inspect the offering. Remember, a bluegill is very cautious about what he puts in his mouth, and that caution increases with age.

Some warm-water ponds host massive emergences of Chironomid midges in mid-summer. We don't fish the actual emergence, which occurs at night, but concentrate on the pupal phase in the days preceding the actual hatch. Countless millions of larvae rise into the surface film where they assume their pupal form. The water is absolutely alive with them—you have to wash them off your tube and waders. The bluegills react to this by forming small, wedge-shaped schools, which move around the pond in a serpentine and unpredictable way as the fish consume large quantities of protein-rich larvae. This schooling activity will occur only in the morning, before the surface gets too hot, but may continue all day under overcast or rainy conditions. This creates a classic "secondary hatch" of juvenile bream and baitfish drawn from the protective cover into open water. The bulk of the pond's bluegill population will join the visible schools, along with numerous minnows, fry, and other baitfish, but the bass and big bream tend to ignore the larvae and feed instead on the abundance of baitfish.

The angler is, therefore, given the option of addressing the primary hatch with a tiny dry or the secondary hatch with a streamer or diver. Perhaps because of my cold-water background, I enjoy the dry-fly aspects, despite the fact that I would take better fish with a streamer. I

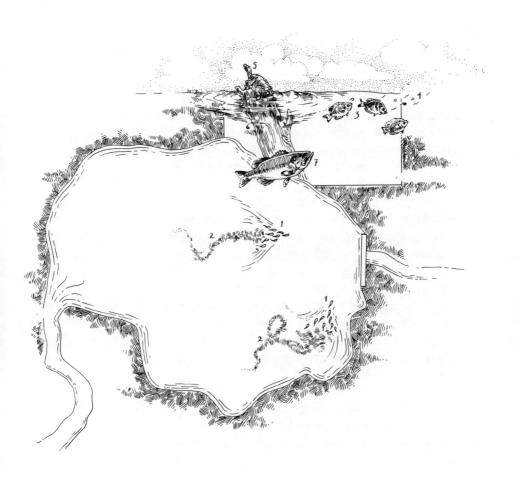

KEY: 1—*wedge-shaped school of bluegill*   5—*basking turtle*
         2—*serpentine course of school*   6—*stump*
         3—*bluegill slurping pupa*   7—*big bass watching*
         4—*midge pupa*   *school of bluegill*

Bluegills form wedge-shaped schools when feeding on midge pupae.

have all season to sink flies to big bream and bass, but this sort of dry-fly opportunity only happens occasionally. Fat, aggressive six-inch bluegill on two-weight tackle and size 18 dries is just too much fun to resist!

These schools are very easily spooked. The water is clear by mid-summer and predatory activity is high. Sometimes a kingfisher will dive into a school right in front of you, a blue catfish will sweep in from behind with his mouth wide open, or a lunker bass will spoil your plans with a huge splash. Effective dry-fly presentation requires long, accurate casts; you have to put the fly directly in front of the moving school while remaining outside of their window of vision. The low profile of a float tube allows you to get closer than with a boat, but fifty- to sixty-foot casts are still the rule. Any error at all will likely spook the whole school; the fly has to land, with the tip-pet straight, within a little two-foot semi-circle in front of the visible fish. This is made all the more difficult by the fact that the school is moving quite rapidly and following completely unpredictable courses; they may turn ninety degrees to the right or left or suddenly make a 180-degree turn and go away from you. You can't make a cast from behind a school without lining them. Maneuvering the tube into position takes skill, practice, and luck. This is really very challenging and each fish will represent considerable effort. "Why go to all that trouble just to catch a little bream?" my neighbor asked, but I'm quite confident that all my readers know the answer to that question.

Craneflies are also abundant in southern waters, but I associate them with the cooler water conditions of spring and fall. They are more of a factor on creeks and tailwaters than on ponds and lakes. I fish for spotted bass in a local tailwater river each November. Early in the morning, before the gates are opened and the big generators start rolling, the bass are chasing threadfin shad right below the dam. One recent morning I arrived before the crack of dawn and could hear the fish feeding. I threw my reliable Marabou Muddler at them for thirty frustrating minutes without a take. With more daylight, I could see the big cranefly larvae in the water. I switched to a big, slow-sinking larval pattern and took fish steadily for the next hour. I can't explain why a normally opportunistic feeder would ignore the shad and zero in on those larvae. Perhaps they are an "easier" meal—the fish don't have to chase them. In any case, entomology can be as important to the warm-water angler as it is to the trout fisher.

THE ODONATANS

These beautiful insects occur in every size and color in warm waters. Some species, like the black damsel with its luminescent blue-green body, are absolutely breathtaking. As the season progresses, each species will have its time on the pond. We see the chartreuse-and-black clearwings in spring and with warming weather rust-colored amberwings and red skimmers begin to appear. The lovely little blue damsel is the harbinger of fall in East Texas. When the fish aren't cooperating, the angler is entertained by the courtship and hunting antics of these agile flyers. One evening a squadron of large dragonflies decided to attack the cloud of mosquitoes that's always around my repellent-protected head. The huge insects would dive right at my face at high speed, just like fighter planes, and veer away at the last second, mere inches from my eyes. This went on for some time and was quite an unnerving experience. They are ferocious predators and belong, in fact, to the only order of insects that actually have teeth (which they never use to bite people). The unusual sight of a bass leaping into the air to take a hovering dragonfly has been much portrayed on canvas. It is always thrilling to witness. But so far, I haven't figured out a way to hover my fly in the air.

East Texas fly fishers Lynn O'Bannion and Rebecca Cooper were casting adult dragonfly patterns to small bass on the Angelina River one recent afternoon when Lynn snagged something on the back cast that nearly jerked the Sage 690 out of his hand. Rebecca gasped. She had seen a bass in the five-pound class leap out of the water to grab the artificial dragonfly during its microsecond pause at the end of the back cast. When Lynn spun around he somehow got the line under the boat and subsequently lost the fish when it tangled around the motor. Lynn is inclined toward Irish hyperbole, but Rebecca is a media executive with a deep commitment to journalistic integrity; her veracity is unquestioned. Maybe he can learn to do this consistently on the fore cast and develop a new technique for us!

While the adults of smaller species of Odonatans are regularly taken by bream, we are more concerned with the nymphal forms. They don't emerge *en masse*, as we shall see in Chapter 5, and flies that imitate adult dragonflies have never been very productive for me—until recently. I had fished them dead still on the water, assuming that I was imitating the spent female, and I couldn't understand why they failed to interest many bass or large bream. Such patterns should be very productive, considering the abundance of these insects, and I erroneously assumed that I wasn't tying them right. I discovered last summer that instead of imitating the spent female with a motionless presentation, I should address the behavior of the occasional adult that gets trapped in the surface film (quite unusual for these strong fliers). I had been lax in my observations and decided to devote an afternoon to that end. I learned that the trapped dragonfly will struggle mightily to regain the air for a few moments and then rest for a long period. He thrashes the surface with his useless, waterlogged wings, but makes little or no lateral headway. This may continue for several minutes, punctuated by long rests, before it attracts the attention of a game fish. I mimic this with several very short, noisy retrieves, moving the fly laterally only a few inches, and then letting it sit for a count of thirty. It's slow fishing, but I've been taking some nice fish that way. The bass may watch the natural insect for a very long time, and a fish always seems to strike when the fly recommences movement after a long rest period. One of the toughest challenges of warm-water fly fishing is trying to make an imitation struggle without swimming it.

MAYFLIES

As noted above, the Ephemeroptera are nowhere near as important in warm water as they are to the cold-water trout fisher. Nonetheless, we do have some impressive hatches of big Hexagenia on certain muddy-bottomed well-oxygenated lakes. This is the same huge, green drake of Michigan trout streams and other midwestern waters. In addition to this common slate-colored insect, we also see the gorgeous golden mayfly in the Deep South. Both of these insects are well imitated by the Rat-Faced McDougal, in appropriate colors.

Smaller mayflies, probably of the Baetidae group, also emerge in comparatively small numbers from a few lakes and ponds in the very early spring. When these insects are emerging on a sunny afternoon in March, the angler is in for a treat. My wife and I spent a delightful afternoon on a large private lake near Crockett, Texas, this past spring. We had taken a number of bass from the still cool water, but we were a little disappointed that the big bluegills we knew to be there had made themselves scarce. We assumed that the water was still too cold for them. I was placing the rod tubes in the trunk when Darlene picked up a mayfly from the top of the car. We both admired it—we like mayflies—and then noticed quite a lot of the brown duns in the air. After the third rise on the cove we had just left, we knew we had to re-rig the rods. Those bream were *big*, and we took a number of them on size 12 Adams dries before darkness fell. It was dry-fly fishing of the very best kind, but such classic situations are not the norm in warm water.

Lake Steinhagen in Tyler County, Texas, is fifteen minutes from our home and hosts two or three massive Hexagenia emergences each June—and I mean massive. Shoreside branches droop into the water with the weight of countless thousands of resting duns, and on the second day the air is so full of spinners that they create a traffic hazard on a nearby bridge. The insects are so thick that you can't comfortably run a boat across the lake. On the last day, great rafts of spent wings line the banks and weed beds. On the first day, everything in the lake is feeding on the emerging duns, but during the spinner phase the mayflies seem to be completely unmolested. There are millions of spinners on the water, but you can't buy a strike on the second day. I assume the fish become satiated and are just lying on the bottom digesting, as warm-water fish are inclined to do. You have to be there on the first day to enjoy good fishing.

In response to complaints from boaters and casting-rod anglers the Corps of Engineers drained the lake this winter to kill excessive vegetation. At this writing, they are refilling it and it should be fishable in the spring. The fish have survived in the river channel as planned—at least those the bait-fishers missed—but I'm terribly concerned about the mayflies. Hopefully a few nymphs were able to follow the receding water to the river or found enough moisture to keep the hatch alive.

CRUISING BLUEGILLS ON THE DRY

Dave Whitlock has said that big summer bluegills are harder to catch than big trout. When these fish leave the security of the depths to hunt for food in the shallows, they are very skittish indeed and require all the persistence and skill the angler can muster. They may be completely opportunistic on these feeding forays, but don't forget the discernment factor. They will examine your offering very carefully. If it doesn't pass inspection, it will be rejected. Now, understand that the fish use different criteria than we do—they may turn down a beautifully tied dry and accept some ratty-looking mess from the trash can at the beginner's fly-tying class. I don't pretend to second guess the fish in that area. Rest assured, however, that the mature bluegill looks carefully at everything he eats.

Bluegills don't surface-feed very often and are best approached with nymphs and streamers most of the time. They do rise occasionally, however, usually for a large terrestrial—a hopper, large beetle, wasp, or bumble bee, floating caterpillar, etc. They will often cruise the shallows in the very early morning, searching for Odonata nymphs, minnows, and all sorts of crustaceans. They are vulnerable to a large dry at that time, and there is nothing like the spectacular rise of a one-pound bluegill at the crack of dawn. The first light of day is a magical time for the farm-pond angler. One feels completely in harmony with the awakening world, utterly alone yet not lonely. When one of these big, orange-breasted fellows shatters the calm, steaming surface to grab a well-tied, well-presented hopper imitation, the angler enjoys one of the great rewards of the fly-fishing experience.

Sometimes large cruising bluegills will be seen moving along a weed-line in the middle of the day. Usually in small groups, they will cruise banks adjacent to deep water, such as levees or creek channels. They are very alert at such times and are virtually unapproachable from the water. Even the hint of a disturbance on the pond will send them scurrying for the depths, and if they see any movement on the bank they will quickly disappear. If I see a group without their seeing me, I will note

the direction they are going and sneak down the bank for some distance ahead of them. The weedline is normally quite narrow on steep levee banks and I will present an appropriate dry—whatever is around at the time—about a foot beyond the edge of the weeds. Only the tippet is exposed; the leader butt and fly line will by lying on the weeds or on the bank. A bow-and-arrow cast is often called for here. I will remain absolutely still, and when I see the fish approaching, I will jiggle the fly *slightly* to imitate a struggling insect. If I'm lucky, one big fellow will leave the little group, rise up under the fly, and inspect it for five to ten seconds. If he decides it's edible, he will snatch it and head for the middle of the pond. If he doesn't find a snag, break the tippet, or get in the moss, I may be able to wear him out enough to drag him over the weedbed and land him.

Mature bream undergo a Jekyll and Hyde transformation of personality in late spring and early summer. After the bass have consummated their annual tryst, and the water temperature is well into the seventies, the male bluegill will move into the shallows to prepare a nuptial bed for his lady fair. This normally intelligent, discerning creature now throws caution to the wind and becomes a complete sucker for any offering (like many young fly fishers when similarly engaged).

Big, cruising bluegills can be incredibly spooky.

He excavates the nest, invites the female to lay her eggs, and zealously protects them until they hatch. He will continue to guard the fry for a couple of days before seeking the depths to recuperate, and he will savagely attack anything that comes near, including a neighboring spawner, with reckless abandon. The only freshwater fish that manifests greater courage in the discharge of his parental obligations is the Rio Grande perch. That small member of the tropical Cichlid family will actually bite an angler on the leg if he wades too close! The bluegill doesn't go quite that far, but he will hold his ground when you approach; trembling with fear, he will turn to watch your every move. The fish are extremely vulnerable to predation at this time and many are taken by otters, herons, and anglers. Fortunately, an individual fish is only thus exposed for about a week. This brief period of aggressive behavior masks the bluegill's wary nature the rest of the year and is responsible, along with his widespread distribution in diverse habitats, for his undeserved reputation as "easy." All species of sunfish spawn in this same basic manner, although they may vary in temperature preference, water depth, types of cover, and bottom characteristics. They all bed communally and, although some natural hybridization does occur, species don't readily mix.

Bluegills return to the same bedding area year after year. As discussed in Chapter 2, the angler should scout the edges of a big lake during low-water periods to locate spawning beds for future reference, and the observant pond fisher will also be aware of these bedding areas on his home waters. When fishing unfamiliar waters in late spring and early summer, one can often observe the beds from the bank, if terrain permits, or simply search the shallows with a small bug. Bluegills are more inclined to spawn in open water than are bass. They are especially fond of high spots surrounded by deeper water; as a matter of fact, a big bluegill will never be too far from deep water. In larger lakes, for reasons that are still unclear to me, they may spawn in six to eight feet of water and can only be approached with a sink-tip. In smaller ponds and creeks they will invariably nest in shallow areas. The instant the fly lands on the water above a nest it will be attacked but not necessarily taken. The fish may just slap the fly with his tail in an attempt to knock it away; as a result, the angler thinks that he's reacting too slowly. Although a bait fisherman can virtually clean out an entire bed, the action usually stops for us after a couple of fish. Then we have to rest the bed for a while.

The bluegill is still a very intelligent fish, even in the throes of passion, and gets "wise" to the fly after watching several of his fellows bite the dust. I once observed a bed from the bank while another angler fished it from a tube. After the first fish was hooked, the spawners became extremely agitated. The male bluegills began circling their nests frantically; they knew they were under attack, but could not immediately ascertain the direction and source of the threat. It was a rather pitiful thing to watch. The released fish returned directly to his nest and darted back and forth wildly. When the fly landed again above the bed, it was taken by another nervous fish, who also returned to the pandemonium upon release. When the fly was cast a third time, it was observed by the still circling males, but was not taken. The defensive circling continued for a short while, but after things settled down, the fly lay on the water unmolested. Sometimes you can catch a half-dozen fish off the bed (perhaps only one), but this basic scenario always seems to apply. If the spawners are small (I have seen four-inch fish spawning), they will often continue to take the fly until exhausted. I once took the same poor little fish four times; upon each release he would return to his nest and take the fly again. It was so heart-rending that I finally left him alone. I suspect that he might have continued taking the fly until he died from exhaustion.

I used to look forward to the springtime spawning season, but my enthusiasm for that fishing has waned as my knowledge and respect for the fish have increased. In my early days in the South I restricted my fishing to the spring months. That was the only time I could catch nice bluegills, and in my ignorance I assumed that the season was over in June. Little did I know that the real bream fishing had not yet begun; the serious fly fisher will find the feeding fish of summer and fall far more interesting and challenging than molesting the poor creatures during their mating time.

Bass spawn earlier than bream, but their behavior is quite similar. I once waded back into a shallow spawning area at Lake Sam Rayburn in Texas. Those fish invariably nest in very shallow backwaters that are not accessible to the bass boats. The water was knee-deep and the bedding area was well-concealed behind a line of willows. There were spawning bass everywhere. I was spooking fish off their nests, afraid I would step on the eggs, and felt quite uncomfortable with my intrusion. Although I had a rare opportunity to observe the actual mating ritual, it was not an enjoyable experience and I never returned. Although I still cannot resist the temptation to cast to any sunfish nest, I increasingly feel that I am taking advantage of an unfair situation. I would rather catch one wary feeder than a dozen reckless spawners.

TERRESTRIAL PHENOMENA

There is such a mind-boggling array of insects in the southern ecosystem that entomology soon becomes a passion in its own right. Initially, my interest in these fascinating invertebrates was restricted to the vise, but my studies are increasingly assuming an identity of their own, without regard for the fly-fishing implications. Dallas fly fisher Jeff Hines and I recently saw an adult regal moth for the first time. We had observed her horned larvae in hickory trees and were ecstatic to see this gorgeous, orange-and-yellow adult. It was nearly as exciting as catching a trophy fish!

Since these ponds and creeks are normally surrounded by lush foliage, any terrestrial species can, and occasionally does, find its way into the water. The creative tier can take inspiration from any insect he observes, secure in the knowledge that the local sunfish have probably seen it too. These fish are quite accustomed to strange organisms on the water and are not intimidated by enormous, vividly hued moths or a spider with a six-inch leg span. This understandable acceptance of bizarre terrestrials has encouraged the sustained use of nondescript attractor flies and has prevented fly fishers from applying standard entomological principles to the warm-water fishery. There seemed to be no pragmatic justification for us to concern ourselves with the intricacies of the warm-water food chain. Indeed, such refinements are not required to catch a nice mess of panfish, or trout for that matter, but the angler who fails to study and observe the world in which his prey resides is not only out of tune with nature, he is also depriving himself of the deep spiritual and intellectual rewards that fly fishing should provide. There is far more to this avocation than just catching fish.

DRINKING WASPS AND RAFTING ANTS

These irascible insects command respect from fisher and fish alike. Many wasps, bees, and ants make their home in the southern woods. I haven't begun to identify the myriad species that I see every day. They come in all colors, sizes, and shapes, and range from the industrious leaf-cutter ants tending their underground fungi farms to the viciously aggressive bald-faced hornet. They undergo a complete metamorphosis and are the only insects that have the front and hind wings joined together—hence, the name *Hymen-* (the Greek god of marriage) and *-optera* (wing). Some occupy very narrow and specific niches in the ecosystem, preying only upon certain insects or spiders, whereas others utilize a wide variety of vegetable matter and nectars. Although some communal species may be very aggressive in defense of home and hearth, they are quite docile while gathering nectar or hunting prey. Many inflict a painful sting, which can be life-threatening to some people, and a large quantity of venom will kill anyone. The ground-dwelling velvet ant—the infamous "cow killer" of Texas—is by far the worst of the lot. The large, colorful female packs a horrible wallop, which is not lethal as the old wives claim, but is painful enough to make one wish he were dead! I've experienced only one velvet ant sting (it was hiding in the dog's coat when I petted her), and it was a terrible experience—many times worse than any bee or hornet sting! I'm usually immune to Hymenoptera venom, but I came very close to visiting the emergency room that night. Other insects in the order may present a fearsome appearance, such as the mud-dauber wasp, but are quite harmless. These communal insects are extremely abundant in the warm, humid south and play a major role in our fishery. Their imitations are an important component of the warm-water arsenal. The southern angler who frequents farm ponds and creeks will certainly suffer occasional stings—there's no avoiding it—but it's not a serious matter for most people. Those who have a life-threatening allergic reaction should probably avoid these waters and the woods that surround them.

I see bream taking bees and wasps all the time, and I have always wondered how they could tolerate being stung in the mouth or stomach. I discussed this with Gary Borger and he said that the take was so quick that the insect was probably instantly disabled, which prevented the fish from being stung. He went on to explain that trout appear to like the pungent, acidic taste of ants and that warm-water species may crave these insects for the same reason. Cold-water anglers have long recognized that trout love ants, and Dr. Edward Hewitt actually tasted one himself! (See Gary Borger's *Naturals*, pp. 157–161, for a thorough discussion of this.) Judy Lehmberg, a biology professor as well as an award-winning fly tier, added that some birds also seem to enjoy the formic-acid taste that characterizes the order, and they may even dust their wings in a fire ant mound, inviting stings. In any case, flies that imitate these insects are deadly on any warm-water pond, and several specific phenomena are of special interest to us.

Almost all species of ants annually develop winged males that swarm from the colony in an annual dispersal flight when they mate with the airborne queen. The fertilized queen then lands to set up housekeeping, and the spent males fall dying to the ground—or water. The pond is often covered with spent males, triggering heavy feeding activity. These flights normally occur during the hottest part of the day and whenever a pond is covered with rises on a summer afternoon, winged ants are almost always responsible. Trout fishers are quite familiar with these phenomena, but their significance has not been generally recognized in a warm-water context.

One delightful afternoon in 1979, I stumbled onto the annual dispersal flight of fire ants, the largest and most productive of these events. I didn't know it then, but *Solenopsis invicta*, the imported fire ant, flies like clockwork on the first warm day of late winter, which occurs in February on the Gulf Coast. Winged individuals begin to appear in the colonies in November, and I enjoy monitoring their maturation while walking in the barren winter woods.

Giant black carpenter ants also thrive in southern woodlands. This indigenous species swarms on several occasions during the summer. When I see large numbers of rises on a July afternoon I don't have to walk down to the pond to check the hatch; I automatically rig my three-weight with a size 12 Black Ant. I have seen them pouring out of dead trees by the thousands. A stiff breeze will blow half of these weak flyers directly onto the pond, driving the finny residents absolutely berserk. At that time of year, the ants produce secondary "hatches" of baitfish in addition to superb dry-fly action. Since these events tend to occur when the surface temperature is uncomfortable, ant-feeding bream can be fairly selective. There's no need to actually match the naturals, but in the hot midday sun a ballpark approximation is advisable. Remember that the "big fly-big fish" rule applies to warm-water species, so the secret is to use as large a fly as you can, perhaps a size 12. The bream usually will accept an offering several times larger than the natural, and the larger fly will increase your chances for the big bluegills and small bass that are in the area. If you faithfully match the ant, which may require a size 20 imitation, you will probably take only small bream. If you go too large—size 12 seems to be the breaking point—it will likely be rejected when the surface temperature is very hot or very cold. Annual flights of harvester ants, leaf-cutters, and several other native Formicidae, along with similar swarms of winged termites (Isoptera), will also trigger intense feeding activity.

"Beware of floating colonies of fire ants," admonishes the hurricane preparedness instructions on the side of the grocery bag. This venomous Formicid inflicts a painful sting, which in sufficient numbers can result in death. The distinctive, mounded dirt colonies of these unwelcome immigrants now infest the entire South, damaging agricultural equipment, killing newborn calves, endangering small children, and defacing lawns. The bluegill may be the only American that likes this ill-tempered little Latino! (The so-called "Killer Bees," another Brazilian contribution to our native fauna, have now crossed the Rio Grande. We can only hope that their truculent disposition has been greatly exaggerated.)

In its native Amazonian rain forest the fire ant evolved the perfect survival instinct to cope with our frequent Texas floods. When the creek rises and inundates the mound, the workers sacrifice themselves for the good of the whole by forming a raft with their own bodies to support the queen, larvae, and the rest of the colony. The raft floats down the swollen creek until it encounters an object—including a floating fly line—that the ants can crawl up on. Their downstream progress is often checked by a fallen tree or other debris, and I once watched for hours as workers laboriously carried each larva along a horizontal trunk to dry land and frantically began building a new formicary. Although I have no affection for these aggressive creatures, I cannot help but admire their industry. I never cease to be amazed by the tenacious procreative instincts with which He seems to have imbued all living organisms.

The raft ("ant ball" in the local vernacular) is obviously very vulnerable, and the finny residents of the creek take full advantage of it. Water movement is often apparent as bream feed at their leisure. Fish neither charge headlong into the main mass of insects as one would expect, nor gulp large numbers of these ants; rather, they feed slowly and deliberately. A bluegill will take an individual ant, then back away from the raft and return a few minutes later for another. I once observed an uneducated little bass mouth a grape-sized cluster of live fire ants. His gills flared and his whole body quivered; he blew the ants out and began swimming rapidly in circles, finally settling to the bottom to recover. Apparently, Hymenoptera venom is like alcohol—it must be taken with moderation. Because this only happens during flood conditions, the creek may be murky or even downright muddy, but a dry fly placed near the raft will find a willing taker. No need to match anything here. Go with a big terrestrial; the bream likely will be completely opportunistic at this time. If the raft seems to be surrounded by little sunfish, a larger fly may take a nice bass who has his eye on the baitfish.

Since southern waterways become dangerous, muddy torrents during floods, only the most adventurous of anglers will ever see rafting ants on the creek. They are more likely to encounter them on a big impoundment after a tropical deluge dramatically raises the lake, often without roiling the water. Many colonies are thereby inundated and large areas of rafting ants will drift with the wind in open water. As in the creek, most of the activity is on the periphery where small sunfish cautiously take individual insects. I suspect that such moderation is required because of the venomous nature of this species, but I have not been able to confirm that in the literature or in discussions with biologists. Prowling bass are even more likely to be under the rafts in the lake, and a hair bug will often raise a good fish. A streamer will tempt both bream and bass, but hatch-matching dries will probably take only small sunfish on either the lake or the creek.

Fire-ant rafts were a major concern to Texans during the devastating Christmas floods of 1991, and local TV stations issued nightly warnings to residents of affected areas. The ants are extremely angry when they are forced to raft; they are desperate to regain terra firma and will savagely attack any living thing they contact. The wading or tubing angler must avoid any contact whatsoever with floating colonies. I have had them travel along the fly line and down the rod to my hand only to realize that if I were to place the tube against the raft, the ants would be all over me in seconds—down inside my waders, in my ears and nostrils, and everywhere else! This is no joke—the panic that ensues from thousands of viciously stinging insects may result in drowning, and sustained contact can deliver a lethal dose of venom. The only escape is to drop out of the tube, slip beneath the surface, and swim underwater to a safe place—but that's a lousy alternative if you're wearing waders and a heavy vest! Cast to floating rafts with extreme caution. Keep your eyes open and don't inadvertently back the tube into a raft while playing a fish.

Many species of wasps and hornets construct complex structures to shelter their larvae. Some, such as the mud dauber and thread-waisted wasp, build houses of mud; others chew leaves and bits of wood into a kind of paper-maché that they form into a surprisingly durable hive. Such hanging nests are a common sight in the southern woods. The common red wasp (Vespidae) is extremely abundant around southern waters. On some lakes and swamps, virtually every stick-up, even far from shore, will have a sizable nest by mid-summer. A group of females builds a circular, open-cell structure, which they attach to a branch, stump, or the eaves of a building. There may be hundreds of these nests along the banks of a typical woodland pond by mid-summer, and the brown-red insects constantly drop to the water to drink. They require a great deal of water to chew wood and leaf pulp into paper.

Bluegills spend the whole day trying to catch them, but the wasps are quicker than the fish. They either see the bream coming or, more likely, somehow feel the movement of water beneath their feet and invariably take off just before the fish breaks the surface. The bream do catch a few, enough to keep them interested, and the hapless insect that gets trapped in the surface film is, of course, instant history. This activity is so much fun to watch that I sometimes forget to fish! Obviously, an appropriate dry fly, presented beneath the nest, will bring an exciting rise when this activity is occurring in early summer. I tie a variation of the Rat-Faced McDougal for this (see Wasp McDougal in the fly-tying chapter). The angler who fishes too fast and moves too rapidly along the shoreline will fail to observe this and other phenomena. His very presence may, in fact, temporarily halt the activity, which will resume if he simply slows down and patiently watches.

Unfortunately, grandaddy bluegill has become too wise to play this foolish game of cat and mouse; picking up slow-moving Odonata nymphs in the security of the weedbed is a lot safer and more efficient. Older, wiser bluegills tend to fall for the dry fly only during the spawn

Bluegills and red wasps play a game of cat and mouse all summer.

and occasionally on early-morning feeding forays. The angler who becomes obsessed with big fish, however, will miss out on the many delightful dry fly opportunities available in warm waters. The common
"hand-sized" bream that do chase drinking wasps are still lots of fun on
light tackle. Local bait fishermen take advantage of this phenomenon. A
few uninformed individuals spray the nest with insecticide, causing the
saturated wasps to fall dead on the water—thereby chumming up the
bream, which overlook the foul spray in their feeding frenzy. When I see
someone engaging in this nefarious practice, I try to explain the effects of
introducing such toxins into the environment. Young people seem to understand, but the old-timers generally reject my pleas for restraint. Unfortunately, many older folks in the rural South still view such concerns as
"hippie stuff," and my Yankee accent doesn't help change their minds.
Our public schools, despite their many faults, are at least making children
aware of the environment.

Since a float-tubing angler is quite helpless and unable to flee from a
swarm of angry wasps, the best defense is to assume that every bush con-
tains a nest. Most attacks occur when an angler carelessly approaches the
bank in order to retrieve an expensive bass bug from shoreside foliage. It
is much safer to move in slowly, holding the fly line in your hand and vig-
orously shaking the bush from a safe distance, watching very closely for
flying wasps. If you see any, break the tippet and forget the bug! If you do
get involved with a colony while tubing, the only escape is to hit the quick
release and drop out of the tube, completely submerging yourself for a
few seconds. The wasps disappear instantly and do not wait around for
you to emerge. If you're fishing from a boat, there's no problem—just
jump into the normally warm water and submerge yourself for a moment.
When you surface, they'll be gone. Don't follow my example, though. I
once thought I was submerged, but the top of my head was exposed and
my scalp received countless stings.

When the pond seems dead and I don't know what to use, my favorite
searching pattern is an imitation of the mud dauber wasp. My blue-black
Mud Dauber McDougal (see Chapter 7) will often raise a fish when all
else fails. These insects frequent pond banks all summer, gathering mud to
build their little tubular houses; while they rarely fall into the water, fish
are quite used to seeing them. They provision the nest with spiders for the
developing larvae to eat—not just any spider mind you, but only a certain, specific species! Many Hymenoptera occupy very narrow ecological
niches.

Both honey bees and bumble bees are regular visitors to the gorgeous displays of flowering water plants that grace southern waters each spring. In East Texas the shallows are quite literally buzzing with activity from mid-March until the first of May. Bees are not as adept around the water as the red wasp, and they frequently become trapped in the surface film. A size 12 McGinty or my own Bumble McDougal will bring constant rises at this time. The fly should be fished slowly and without retrieve. Just place the offering near the flowers, jiggle it a little bit, and wait; keep alert though—old grandaddy bluegill may smash it at any moment! Smaller bass often fall for Hymenoptera imitations as well. I sometimes enjoy veritable "hatches" of honey bees in the early spring. An apiary company from North Dakota places hundreds of hives in the woods a short distance from my ponds for winter storage. They pick them up in April and transport them all over the country for orchard pollination, but the bees fly by the thousands on every pleasant winter day. Their numbers are often sufficient to stimulate surface-feeding activity.

HOPPERS AND KIN

Countless hordes of small toothpick and meadow grasshoppers, along with the wingless nymphs of larger species, keep farm-pond bream well supplied with protein on the windy days of spring. Most of these little hoppers, including most nymphal forms, are green in color and really too small to tie in the preferred Whitlock-style; the old Joe's Hopper design is more adaptable for tiny springtime hoppers. The small hoppers are poor fliers and the nymphs can't fly at all—they are at the mercy of the wind during airborne leaps. They jump ahead of the legs of cattle, horses, or other animals; if this occurs on the windward side of the pond, many are blown into the water. A grazing animal may be accompanied by a whole school of feeding bream as it forages along the bank. When I see that situation, I kick the tube at top speed to the area before the animal moves away.

Many mature hoppers may be blown onto the pond by the gusty winds of October. Such was the case one recent afternoon. Big bream were rising steadily to naturals, and my hand trembled as I threaded a 4X tippet through the eye of a size 8 Dave's Hopper. To my dismay, the husky bluegills refused this and several other hopper imitations, maddeningly taking naturals within inches of my offering. Every time I picked up the fly there was a swirl behind it; the fish were examining and rejecting my phoney hoppers. After thirty frustrating minutes, I collected a dozen real grasshoppers in the surrounding meadow, left my rod on the bank so I couldn't be accused of chumming, and paddled back to the area. The fish took some of the drifting naturals that I threw on the water, but refused others. Hoppers that I had handled too roughly and had died were not taken; the fish inspected them, as they had my fly, but only live, kicking insects were actually eaten. Subsequent efforts to impart such struggling action to a variety of patterns failed. It was classic dry-fly refusal and as difficult as any comparable situation on cold water.

The naturals were still present when Jeff Hines and Bob Johnson, both skillful trout fishers, arrived a few days later. I described the problem to them and they were in their tubes within minutes. We studied the kicking motion of the struggling insects as they drove themselves forward in short darts. Jeff and I believed that the key was in the movement of the powerful back legs, but Bob suspected that my hoppers, with their clipped deer-hair heads, were creating an unnatural disturbance when retrieved. He dug deep in his box and found a Henry's Fork Hopper (a bullet-head pattern created by Idaho guide Mike Lawson) and took big bream the rest of the evening while Jeff and I watched admiringly. Although it's only vaguely suggestive of a grasshopper, the movement of water around the smooth head was more realistic and Bob could retrieve it in short jerks without spooking the fish. Mike Lawson has kindly given me permission to reprint his tying instructions in Chapter 7. This experience, along with the dragonfly incident related above, demanded that I revise my previous assumption that terrestrials should *never* be retrieved. Many such revisions are sure to follow as we develop this exciting and dynamic fly-fishing frontier.

Grasshoppers are powerful swimmers and quite agile on the water's surface. It is apparent that they are trying to reach shore when they land on the pond. They remain still for a moment to get their bearings and then make a bee-line for the bank or a nearby object. They clearly know exactly where they are going and seem to be aware that they are in mortal peril. Many actually make it, dry their wings, and appear none the worse for wear. Bluegills don't chase them—that would be very "un-bluegill-like" indeed—rather, they follow behind and snatch the hopper only when it stops to rest. Those insects that don't stop survive. This is another cat-and-mouse game between fish and insect. All predators are aroused by fleeing prey, and the bluegill is no exception. Florida angler Dana Griffin has observed one genus of Orthoptera, *orchelinum* (sometimes called "meadow katydid"), that can swim underwater and actually does so to evade predatory birds! Dana represents the new breed of warm-water angler—observant, studious, and ecologically oriented—that I hope our sport will evolve in coming years. His Diving Hopper imitates

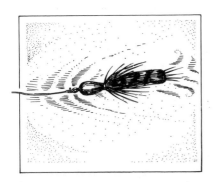

A bullet head hopper pattern moves smoothly through the water.

orchelinum, and the tying instructions will be found in *American Angler* (May/June, 1992).

As the season progresses, more drably colored, larger hoppers begin to appear. These are best represented by Dave's Hopper on sizes 6 to 10. They don't find their way into the water as frequently as do the smaller insects, but a hopper pattern is always a good choice all summer for larger bass as well as bream. This is an excellent pattern for cruising bluegills or early-morning feeders, especially on ponds that are surrounded by pasture or hayfields. The grasshopper is, of course, a grassland insect and is not much of a factor in woodland ponds and creeks.

Huge, brightly marked lubber grasshoppers and the giant, migratory bird grasshopper that appears in East Texas after the first cool front of fall do not normally fall in the water, but really big hopper imitations still seem to work well when they are in the area. The southern angular-winged katydid, another Orthoptera, does not fall in the water either, yet chartreuse hair bug imitations are effective when fished under the bushes where they are resting. It's as though the fish somehow know that one could possibly fall in the water. An insect doesn't necessarily have to actually be in the water to warrant the angler's attention.

Spent female cicada are a common sight on these waters during early summer. This is the common Western Cicada, not the famous seventeen-year variety. This large, beautiful insect crawls out on a small tree limb, scratches a slot in the bark, lays her eggs, and falls spent to the ground—or water. Bass love them and often mistake a natural-and-black size 2 hair bug for a juicy cicada. Some entomologists contend that the cicada doesn't belong in the Orthoptera order, but the Audubon field guide places it in that group—and that's good enough for me.

A clipped deer hair head creates an unnatural commotion when retrieved.

The observant angler will be aware of many lesser phenomena. Predatory lacewings and ladybugs lay their eggs in colonies of willow aphids, and bream take the spent females as they drift down the creek. The carcass of a dead mammal may host large, slow-flying carrion beetles, which may be knocked into the water by quarreling vultures. What appear to be "gnats" on the water may actually be spent acorn weevils or even wind-born spiders. The ecologically oriented trout fisher will find this habitat, with its rich diversity of life, not only a fascinating new laboratory for his studies but a veritable paradise for his angling as well.

AFTER DARK

The serious bass fisher will want to visit the pond at night. Like most southern wildlife, big bass tend to be nocturnal feeders. This requires special skills and intimate familiarity with the waters. Prowling around the woods at night is an unnatural, even frightening, experience for me, but on one recent moonlit night I ventured out into the darkness, armed only with a nine-weight fly rod and a box of hair bugs.

At the pond's edge I was greeted by a cacophony of lovesick frogs, serenading crickets, and clouds of ravenous mosquitoes—all punctuated by the mournful cries of the whippoorwill. An armadillo, preoccupied with his ceaseless digging, nearly bumped into my leg. Raccoons were busily feeding on the dewberry patch, and a solitary doe was silhouetted against the rising moon across the pond. Only at night does one realize how diverse southern wildlife really is. My reverie was rudely broken by a huge splash a few feet down the bank. A hapless frog had been swallowed alive by a huge bass that I would probably never see in the daytime. "This is my chance," I muttered aloud.

I wish I could tell you that I executed a perfect cast and landed an eight-pound trophy for my tying-room wall. The sad truth is that my back cast caught the dewberry patch and scared off the raccoons. My cursing desecrated the tranquil night; the doe fled into the woods, the armadillo scurried into his hole, and even the frogs quit singing. Only the mosquitoes refused to be deterred by my rude expletives. I jerked and yanked angrily, but the 0X tippet held. I tripped over an unseen log, fell face down on the muddy ground, and tore my forearms to shreds on the dewberry thorns. My rod was still intact, but my ego was shattered. I returned to the house a beaten and bloodied man. Chester, my faithful cat, observed the whole unfortunate incident from a nearby stump. Luckily for him, he never uttered a peep.

Night fishing can be extremely productive during the summer, especially for the larger bass, but only seasoned, competent fly fishers with the patience of Job need apply. It can be a maddening and frustrating experience for an expert, an impossible nightmare for a novice. Missed strikes, tangles, snags, and lost fish are par for the course, but the thrill of one of those magnificent fish engulfing a big hair bug, followed by a spectacular leap, is without equal. Always crimp your barbs and avoid stainless hooks, since lost fish are inevitable.

This may raise your eyebrows, but the most productive (and fun) rig for night fishing is a four-inch black plastic salamander ("lizard" in bass fishing parlance) cast on a heavy two-foot leader and a shortened sinking-tip, eight-weight fly line. It is completely weedless, so you don't have to be all that careful about where it lands, it fishes by feel rather than vision, and it is an eminently appropriate offering at night because all species of mud puppies, newts, sirens, and similar amphibians are nocturnal feeders. It's more fun at night than fishing a bug because you don't have so much trouble with it. I crimp the barb on the No. 1 worm hook, because bass sometimes take these baits rather deeply, and I try to strike the fish in a timely manner before he swallows the hook.

It's not hard to cast. In fact, it's easier than a heavily weighted bass fly—once you get used to it. You can fish with flies at night if you want to, but I'm going to use that "lizard." Try it some dark night. You'll become a believer in a hurry!

Stay in areas that you know—this is not the time to explore new waters. I prefer to use the jon boat at night. Although alligators are of little concern during the day, they do become much more aggressive after dark. On waters with very large populations, float tubing is probably inadvisable at any time, but I know local people who "pay them no mind" at all and don't hesitate to get right into the water with them. They are curious creatures; I have had them swim around my tube staring at me. I must confess to a certain feeling of discomfort when they slip beneath the surface, but I have never had one behave in a threatening manner. I can't imagine a finer, more appropriate way for an aging fly fisher to meet his Maker than being consumed by a gator; for his mortal remains to become part of the very ecosystem that he has studied and loved. To play that final role in the timeless drama of predator and prey is a privilege devoutly to be wished. It would be the only meal Mr. Gator ever had that is served with a $400 graphite toothpick! I'm not ready yet, but one way to assure such a fate is to drag a stringer of fish in the water while tubing or wading, especially at night. Unless you enjoy close encounters with a variety of large reptiles, including the huge, vicious loggerhead turtle, *never* drag fish around. Most snakes are also nocturnal, but please don't allow irrational fear to spoil your fun. Snakes are timid creatures and we certainly don't represent prey to them. Unless you bait them with a fish, step on one, or stick your hand in a hollow log, there is little to fear. Moreover, the few bites that do occur, when properly treated, aren't really that serious. The biggest danger is driving in panic to the doctor!

Far more dangerous to the night fisher is the possibility of motorboat traffic. Always have a powerful flashlight ready at hand to warn an oncoming craft of your presence. There is nothing romantic in being chopped up by a propeller! Finally, you definitely must not forget the insect repellent on a night outing!

So, if you can cast like Gary Borger, have the ability to tie a Duncan loop blindfolded, can afford to lose a couple of dozen bugs in a single night, have the courage to stare down a hungry alligator, and own stock in Cutter Laboratories, night bass fishing may be your bag!

4

THE REST OF
THE MENU

Little wonder that southern game fish feed so opportunistically; consider the vast array of food available to them! Dozens of species of baitfish, all sorts of amphibians, reptiles, and a long list of freshwater crustaceans provide the fly tier and amateur naturalist alike with a mind-boggling array of life forms to observe, study, and imitate. This variety should not delude the tier into assuming that warm-water fish don't demand the same kind of care ordinarily put into trout flies. He should bear in mind that these fish are intelligent and discerning.

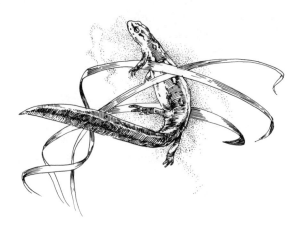

Adult Newt

A little knowledge can go a long way. For instance, some naturalists believe that predatory fish can distinguish between newts and other salamanders; the fish avoid the former because of their toxic secretions. If true, that represents a very sophisticated level of discernment that must be taken into consideration when you tie a pattern. Rather than rely on a generalized fly designed to imitate the entire group—a pattern that may prove to be entirely ineffective—you can customize your offerings with external gills, which are an exclusive feature of the non-toxic salamanders.

Likewise, if most of the frogs in and around a given farm pond are two-inch-long chorus frogs with a cream ventral and gray dorsal, wouldn't a size 2 natural hair bug make better sense than a 2/0 black-and-yellow offering? Yes, oversized attractor lures will take bass, and Mepps spinners are deadly on rainbows. My point is that a real understanding of the life processes of the fish and their prey will greatly enhance your enjoyment while on the water by putting you in tune with nature—and the knowledge so gained is also a fundamental part of the philosophy of fly fishing.

REPTILES AND AMPHIBIANS

Many species of salamanders—waterdogs, mud puppies, newts, sirens, and hellbenders—abound in warm waters. Many of these amphibians are thoroughly aquatic and undoubtedly account for the phenomenal success of plastic worms and "lizards" as bass baits. These bizarre-looking creatures range in size from a few inches to a couple of feet in length and are at the very top of the bass' list of food preferences. Even a lethargic, non-feeding fish cannot resist a fleshy, easily caught, bottom-crawling salamander.

Though theoretically it is possible to imitate these organisms with flies constructed with strips of rabbit hide, chamois, saddle hackles or dubbed wool, my attempts to do so have been somewhat disappointing. Perhaps I'm expecting too much by comparing their performance to that of the soft-plastic salamanders. Those molded lures are just so incredibly effective (for reasons that we'll discuss in Chapter Five) that it is becoming increasingly difficult for me to justify the use of flies for lethargic, bottom-grubbing bass—especially since I have discovered that the smaller baits handle very nicely on the fly rod. Some fly fishers cast tiny polymer grubs to deep bream. Worse, some use plastic salmon eggs to take trout, but I draw the line there. God had the split-cane purist in mind when He made the trout, and He had the Southern Baptist fly rodder in mind when He made the bluegill. But He was thinking of neither when He created old Mr. Bigmouth!

An equally large number of frogs and toads inhabit warm, southern waters and adjacent land areas. The adults come in all sizes and colors, but I suspect that they are more important as fish food in the larval phase. Nonetheless, most of our bass bugs and topwater casting lures are designed to represent adult amphibians. An understanding of their life cycles and habits, coupled with some basic knowledge of the differences in species, will not only enhance the rewards we derive from our sport, but probably lead to improved fly patterns and more fish on the line.

The most important group to us is probably the family Hylidae—a large group of small frogs which includes the tree frogs, cricket frogs, and the noisy chorus frogs that are so abundant around southern ponds. Rarely exceeding one and a half to two inches in length, their dorsal coloration varies among species from drab browns and grays to vivid chartreuse with bright yellow lines. The ventral side is almost always light yellow or white, but may have dark markings in some species. These are the shy little fellows that we hear but never see. Since most of the hair bugs that we tie represent frogs of the Hylidae family, they are as worthy of our attention as are the mayflies in a trout stream.

Observation and collection is best done at night with the aid of a flashlight, but watch out for snakes when poking around the pond after dark. Frogs and toads are also important forage in the juvenile stage. In *Naturals*, Gary Borger presents a little fly called "Tadpolly," which he credits to English angler John Goddard. This is an excellent imitation of the larval phase of these frogs and should, along with Dave Whitlock's tadpole pattern, be included in every warm-water angler's box. Be aware that in parts of the Deep South a "pollywog" is not a frog larvae, but a small bullhead catfish. Such colloquialisms abound everywhere. You can't avoid their use, but keep in mind what each name actually refers to.

Larger frogs often take flies and put up a surprisingly good fight. On a recent outing, my companion took two enormous bullfrogs on a 2/0 natural hair bug. He releases his bass, but the frogs went home. (Many country folks eat the whole frog, not just the back legs.) Some years ago, I was camped in a swamp area when a nearby camper invited me to share some frog legs for supper. He had caught more than he and his family could eat. I gratefully accepted and the fried legs were delicious. I nearly regurgitated dinner, however, while exploring the water's edge with a flashlight later that evening. I was shocked by the horrifying spectacle of a number of bleeding frogs pitifully trying to pull themselves toward the water sans hind legs! That cruel man had removed the legs without bothering to kill the frogs. I dispatched all the poor creatures I could find, then walked to his camp and expressed my displeasure. Fortunately, his children had retired for the night, but his wife was appalled. The next morning I saw him sleeping alone in their nearby boat.

Snakes also thrive in these habitats. Over a dozen species of common water snakes (all of the genus *Natrix*) are of special interest to fly fishers. Usually eight to ten inches long at birth, a juvenile water snake is at great risk in bass water, and patterns that represent them are absolutely deadly where substantial populations occur. For best results, you need to know the coloration of the predominant species in the water you fish. Keep in mind that identification is impossible at a distance, and since young cottonmouths are similar in appearance, care must be exercised when collecting specimens. Belly color, of paramount concern to the fly tier, may be cream, mottled yellow, or yellow with red bands. At least one East Texas species has a green belly and the "copperbelly" of Georgia has a bright red venter. The many species of innocuous garter (*Thamnophis*) and ribbon (*Tropidoclonion*) snakes that frequently hunt in farm ponds are smaller— five to six inches at birth—than the water snakes and more brightly colored.

Absent close examination, darkly colored, harmless water snakes are virtually indistinguishable from the venomous cottonmouth. If you are bitten while collecting, kill the specimen and examine the belly; if there is a double row of scales from the anal plate to the tail, put a Band-Aid on the bite and forget it. On the other hand, if there is only a single row of scales below the anal plate, medical attention is advisable. The easiest way to tell the difference while fishing is in the behavior of the snake. The cottonmouth will hold his ground or make a slow, threatening retreat, but a water snake will flee in panic.

Many southern anglers don't realize that juvenile turtles are frequently taken by bass. Species of the basking genus *Chrysemys*, the common "cooters" and sliders of southern ponds, are extremely abundant and widespread in most warm-water habitat. If nest predation by raccoons, skunks, and snakes hasn't been too heavy, there may be many baby turtles in the water by early summer. The observant angler will see bass rise and take them regularly. I have long suspected that the bass ejects the turtle without swallowing it, and recent research data has confirmed that. Chuck Tryon recently sent me some data that indicate that bass will take a baby turtle one time only, since it bites and claws them severely in the mouth. A young, uneducated fish that actually eats a turtle will die from internal injuries. Though imitating turtles may seem to be counterproductive, my "turtle bugs" still work. Could it be that the bass mistakes my baby turtle for something else? Surely not!

The plastron, or underside, of young turtles have distinctive markings which disappear with age. A juvenile redeared pond slider (*C. scripta elegans*), the most common species in my area, has a bright yellow plastron with distinct black spots; anglers in Alabama and Mississippi may find young sliders with orange-reddish plastrons (*C. concinna hieroglyphica*). Hair bugs with short tails and no hackle are good imitations. Concentrate on the bottom and sides of your hair bugs; after all, those are the only parts the bass sees. All that fancy stacking work on the back is aesthetically pleasing, but it has little effect on the performance of the bug.

THE BAITFISHES

In my area of southeast Texas there are twenty-two kinds of minnows and shiners (Cyprinidae), thirteen kinds of darters (Percidae), four silversides (Athernidae), five species of topminnows (killifish), two separate shad (herring), one abundant little live bearer (*Gambusia affinis*, the common mosquitofish), and six small forage sunfish (flier, spotted, banded pygmy, orange-spotted, dollar, and bantam). Obviously, even the most dedicated match-the-minnow enthusiast can't carry that many patterns, and attempts to do so would be ludicrous. It behooves the serious angler to determine which baitfish are most prevalent in his home water. In my own area, for example, I know that while the Sabine shiner is extremely abundant in the Neches River, it is rarely found in its tributary, Turkey Creek. The redfin shiner abounds in Turkey Creek, but not in the Neches. Several other shiners occur in both waters. This kind of information on local waters, although certainly not essential for angling success, makes the fly-fishing game much more interesting. I daresay that I could catch a few trout on Pennsylvania's famous Yellow Breeches without knowledge of local insect life, but my trip would be far more gratifying if I were somewhat familiar with the food forms in the creek. There is no reason why the warm-water angler cannot similarly arm himself with such data.

Although one lightly colored streamer may represent a number of baitfish, certain species have pronounced characteristics and deserve special consideration on the water and at the vise. The red shiner (N. *lutrensis*) is common in most creeks and some ponds that I fish. This minnow is two to three inches long and the male develops blood-red fins and tail in early summer. Therefore, I emphasize red on my Marabou Muddlers for these waters. From reading and observation, I also know that this fish spawns in weedbeds. Hence, I fish a red streamer near weedy areas in early summer. A totally different baitfish may predominate in another pond or creek. A different strategy is required, but the concept is the same. The principles of study, observation, collection, imitation, and presentation, which have been a fundamental element of fly fishing for centuries, apply here, too.

I suggest that the warm-water angler adopt a basic streamer design and simply modify color and size according to the baitfish he expects to be present. Dave Whitlock's match-the-minnow design, Matuka-styles, classic featherwings, or even some of the saltwater patterns are adaptable enough to meet our needs. I use the Marabou Muddler myself. Certain baitfish, such as the very large, deep-bodied gizzard shad (D. *cepedianum*) or the six-inch golden shiner (N. *crysoleucas*) require, of course, separate treatment—a six-inch Muddler would be grotesque indeed!

Juvenile sunfish are by far the most important forage in farm ponds, and they play the same basic role as threadfin shad in large, southern reservoirs. Most streamers fail to effectively represent the deep-bodied profile of the sunfish; those that do don't behave properly in the water. Nonetheless, I am certain that bass and big bluegills are mistaking my Muddlers for small bream.

The fry and young of many other fish also constitute important game fish forage at times. I once saw several small bass attempt to dine on a school of bowfin fry. The male bowfin valiantly fought them off; first, he tried to decoy the bass, finally he attacked them. The bass decided that discretion was the better part of valor at this point and made a hasty retreat. Because of their tight schooling behavior, schools of young catfish

Golden Shiner

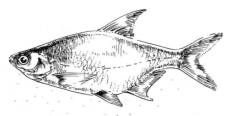

Emerald Shiner

Gizzard Shad

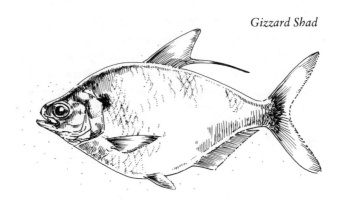

Red Shiner

Some Common Baitfish of the Gulf Coast

are especially vulnerable to bass and bream predation. Papa Catfish, while not as intimidating as the bowfin, does a credible job of protecting his off-spring. These life and death dramas are a part of daily life in the pond, and the angler who fails to observe them and concentrates all of his attention on just catching another fish is depriving himself of the simple pleasures of a day on the water.

CRUSTACEA, MOLLUSCA, AND ANNELIDA

Only two classes in the phylum Crustacea concern us: the Amphipods (scuds) and the Decapods (crawfish and freshwater shrimps). I really know very little about scuds, and I don't tie a pattern to represent them—*yet*. I have gathered from his recent writings that Dave Whitlock uses small scud imitations to take big bream. I do know that scuds are abundant in all the waters we are discussing here (and most everywhere else for that matter) and they likely form an important part of the bream's diet. There are also several species of freshwater shrimps in southern North America, some of them quite large. However, the crawfish is by far the most important crustacean as far as the warm-water fly fisher is concerned.

Crawfish form a large part of the bass' diet in virtually all waters. Although these organisms do have some special mineral requirements, I have found them everywhere. Despite this fact, I rarely fish with crawfish imitations in the cluttered, heavily vegetated waters of East Texas. Such a pattern must crawl along the bottom to be effective. That requires heavy weight, difficult in most southern lakes. A weedguard helps, but moss and debris still gather on the head of the fly. I prefer buoyant flies fished with a short leader on a sinking line, and I restrict such offerings to reptile, fish, and some insect imitations. Moreover, a crawfish swims with a tail-snapping motion that we have never been able to imitate properly. Such patterns are more useful to northern smallmouth and trout anglers, who usually fish in running water; a crawfish that has lost his footing and gets caught in the current is much easier to represent than one that's going about his normal activities in still water.

I am very excited about the warm-water potential of Gary Borger's female crawfish, pictured in *Designing Trout Flies*. He addresses the tail-snapping movement of the organism, and as he points out in *Naturals,* game fish are much more likely to take a fleeing female than a belligerent male with extended claws. I have had early successes with the fly, tying it without lead wire; the combination of the heavy wire Mustad 9672 hook and bucktail wing will achieve near-neutral buoyancy, thereby helping to alleviate snag problems. I use it on a short leader and sinking line.

I occasionally catch crawfish while dredging for insect samples. It's amazing how the coloration of this creature varies with the color of the water. In clear, dark water, they have the brown-orange color that we normally expect, but in muddy water they will be yellow or even cream. They spawn in the winter, and we find females with egg clusters under their tails in January and February. In the spring I find very small, white crawfish and I will sometimes use a white nymph to represent them.

The only mollusks that concern us are the aquatic snails. I find a lot of small snails in my bottom samples, usually black in color and ranging from the size of a pea to a BB. They are the preferred food of the redear sunfish, who is equipped with special grinding teeth in his throat (hence, the colloquial name, "shellcracker") which he uses to break the shells. I have tried the snail pattern presented by Gary Borger on page 207 of his excellent book, *Naturals*. I doubt that Gary intended such warm-water applications of his work, but there has been so little research in our fishery that we have to turn to the cold-water literature for information. He offers both a floating and sinking pattern, and I have had some limited success with the latter, though I'm not sure I'm tying it correctly since it's not pictured in the text. The only realistic application that we have for a snail pattern is the redear sunfish. I believe he will take a nymph as readily as a snail, and the former is much easier to present in a natural manner. I am intrigued by Gary's discussion of a phenomenon that occurs in England; apparently aquatic snails come floating to the surface in the summer for a brief period. The snails are undoubtedly fulfilling some aspect of their life cycle and Gary reports the trout go berserk at such times. I haven't observed this on my waters, but I am watching for it and wouldn't be surprised if it occurs. In any case, a snail imitation is hard to fish in still water; without current to help you, you may grow a long beard waiting for a redear to find the little fly lying in the bottom slime, and a retrieve of any kind hardly seems appropriate. The fish I've taken on a snail fly have probably mistaken it for a poorly tied nymph. I'm waiting for the snails to come floating to the top—I can handle that!

Annelida has only a couple of representatives that concern us: aquatic earthworms and leeches. I haven't found any San Juan worms in my bottom sampling, but leeches are abundant in southern waters. I didn't need bottom samples to learn that, however. I hadn't been in the South long when I decided to wade bare-legged to beat the heat. When

I got out of the tepid creek my legs were covered with leeches. I ran up and down the bank shouting and beating on my infested legs, manifesting much less courage than did Humphrey Bogart in the *African Queen*. I finally regained my composure when I remembered that leeches were once applied medicinally; then I picked them off one by one. When I threw them in the creek, bluegills grabbed them the instant they hit the water! Royce Dam's Strip Leech, also found on page 207 of *Naturals*, is an excellent pattern, although a little too large for our local organisms. If I cut the rabbit strip very thin, however, I can tie it down to a size 8. You may not believe this, but I know some country boys who stand in the creek to gather leeches on their legs for bream bait! The leeches we have in Texas are, surprisingly, much smaller than those I have seen in Idaho's Henry's Lake and in other cold waters.

Gary Borger is the archetypal trout fisher and it is ironic that his works, along with Whitlock's *Guide to Aquatic Trout Foods*, are our best sources of information on many of the aquatic organisms we are attempting to duplicate at the vise. This is, of course, a credit to their scholarship, but also a sad comment on the inadequacies of our own warm-water literature. In any case, *Naturals* is a must on any freshwater angler's bookshelf and the recipes for the above patterns will not be repeated here. I would love to see a trout fisher of Gary's caliber approach our warm-water ponds; I wouldn't be surprised if, in full disguise of course, he already does so in Wisconsin!

5

TO SINK OR
NOT TO SINK

To sink or not to sink, that is the question. The nymph and streamer fisher will take more and larger bream than will the dry-fly purist—and he will do it all season, even during the spawn and in the dead of winter. Like trout, the bulk of the bream's diet comes off the bottom. The rest is made up of small fish, tadpoles, and other swimming organisms at intermediate depths; perhaps ten percent of his total protein intake is consumed off the surface of the pond. In larger lakes mature bream stay deep nearly all the time, and the dry-fly enthusiast will take few quality fish—even big bluegills spawn deep in big southern impoundments.

It seems then quite logical and practical to weight all of our bream flies and present the offering at preferred feeding zones. Fortunately, the act of fly fishing is not a practical pursuit; little of what we do is really logical. On any farm pond in the country an experienced country boy with a can of freshly dug wrigglers can outfish the most skillful fly fisher. No, a real life Mr. Spock would not choose fly fishing as a method of choice, and certainly not dry-fly fishing.

The rest of the story, as a popular radio commentator might put it, is the fact that though topwater fishing is one-tenth as effective, it is ten times more fun. The sight of the surface take, whether a barely visible sip on a Montana spring creek or a crashing splash on a Texas farm pond, is the ultimate angling reward. Sure, it's harder to bring those fish up to the dry. All the better. Sure, you'll catch bigger fish on a streamer.

Who cares? Sure, I've been humiliated by worm-fishing country boys, but I've also taught a few of them to fly fish and to experience the thrill of the rise.

There are, of course, conditions when fishing the dry fly is simply an exercise in futility. Uncomfortable surface temperature, a passing cold front, or poor water visibility all reduce, if not preclude, the likelihood of topwater action. I will not, however, put on a sinking line or weighted fly until I am satisfied that all hope of dry-fly action has been exhausted. This sort of attitude is admittedly self-defeating, but I would rather catch one fish on a dry fly than three on a weighted one. I know that many warm-water fly fishers share this view, as did the genteel trout fishers of yesteryear when Dr. Hewitt began touting the virtues of the nymph. New designs in fly lines have, however, taken a lot of the misery out of deep-water fishing, and we now have the technical capability to present an appropriate bottom-crawling offering to big bass and bream in the zones they frequent most of the time. Nonetheless, we continue to resist these techniques for many of the same reasons that our cold-water progenitors resisted the nymph. Nymphing takes more skill and effort; it offends our aesthetic sensibilities; and most of all it's not as much fun. Perhaps a warm-water incarnation of Edward Ringwood Hewitt will one day change our attitude.

Mature bluegills are remarkably intelligent and discerning. Dave Whitlock has compared them to the wary permit, the ultimate prize of the saltwater fly-rodder and one of the hardest fish in the world to catch. Like still-water trout, big bream most of the time are reluctant to rise to a surface offering. Consistent angling success requires specialized nymphing techniques. The redear is exclusively a bottom-feeder and will rarely, except when spawning, take a dry. Although small bluegills feed on top a great deal and are easily taken, the big fish will rise to a skillfully presented dry only under certain conditions. Since these two species, the largest of the bream, constitute our primary prey, it is obvious that we must overcome our prejudices toward leaded flies. If a former generation of split-cane tweed-clad Victorians could accept the nymph, surely we can too!

NYMPHING IN THE WEEDS

Mature, non-spawning bluegills and redear sunfish feed deep most of the time, and consistent success requires the development of some rather specialized nymphing techniques. There is no current to help us impart natural action to the fly, and we are encumbered by heavy bottom veg-etation, clinging mosses, and all sorts of submerged brush and timber. Warm-water nymphing is considerably more complicated than simply letting the nymph tumble along the bottom of a freestone creek and watching for a pause of the line. Even an unweighted nymph, tradition-ally tied with an exposed hook, is normally impossible to retrieve in the cluttered farm-pond habitat that bream prefer. Such flies must be fished "on the sink" (i.e., anticipating the take while the nymph slowly sinks toward the bottom) or accurately cast to a hole in the surface weeds and slightly "jiggled" while suspended on a floating line or strike indicator. The fly will pick up weeds or moss on every cast, which must be re-moved constantly. The idea of suspending a nymph on a strike indicator is nothing new to the still-water trout fisher who, in the absence of cur-rent, must impart some kind of realistic action to the fly. Add the dis-cerning, spooky nature of the mature bluegill, who leisurely studies every item of food before mouthing it, and you can appreciate why I have been able to catch numbers of big bream only during the spring spawning season.

Dragon and damsel naiads are omnipresent in virtually all waters. They are most abundant in the thickest weedbeds, complicating our presentation problems. The observant angler will notice that dragon-flies almost always lay their eggs in dense vegetation; doing so not only foils the sinister designs of a hungry bass, but also assures an adequate food supply for the newly hatched nymphs who will begin and end their existence in the same weedbed. The nymphs form an important link in the food chain, especially in farm ponds, and their foraging behavior makes them more accessible to fish than burrowing mayfly nymphs.

The Odonata conveniently divide into two suborders—the Anis-optera (dragonflies) and the Zygoptera (damselflies)—which are very different in appearance. Nymphs all share the same drab, brown-olive colorations, but that's where the similarity ends. The damsel naiads are long, slender, delicate insects with three pronounced plumose tails that actually serve as gills. The dragonfly nymphs have wider, flattened ab-domens and no tails (the gills are located, of all places, in the anus). Dragonflies are coarser and larger than damsels, in both the juvenile and adult stages, and I sometimes find nymphs the size of a quarter. I could never understand how the long, slender abdomen of the adult could fit inside the unlikely shaped nymphal husk until I observed one emerge. It seemed to be coiled like a rope inside the husk. The nymphs have huge, shovel-like mouths, and the lower labium extends nearly the length of the body when they snatch a food item. The labium is not usually visible, however, and is not a factor for the fly tier. The adults of all Odonata emerge individually and gradually, rather than *en masse* like many other aquatic insects. Bottom samples will reveal the most prevalent species in a given pond, and the tier will find ample guidance in the cold-water literature. I use variations of Charlie Brooks's Fair Damsel, Polly Rosborough's Casual dress, and the standard Dragon, all found in Terry Hellekson's *Popular Fly Patterns*. Gary Borger is the undisputed fly-fishing authority on this order of insects, and his works are required reading for the serious warm-water enthusiast.

Three aspects of Odonata behavior are of concern to bream fishers. First, they climb plant stems near the bank to undergo their final molt, leaving their nymphal husks behind. This activity occurs very early in the morning, and the insects are vulnerable to bream predation at that time. Bluegills often knock the insect off the stem and then quarrel over it as it tumbles toward the bottom. Nymphs also ascend the stems of water plants while foraging for prey. (They'll also crawl up nearly anything else—rocks, pilings, trotline buoys.) Second, many species are capable of a free-swimming motion—the damsel by undulations of the tails, the

Nymphing for bluegills requires a stealthy approach.

dragon by drawing water into the anus and quickly expelling it. Third, they are often observed crawling along the bottom or waiting in ambush, in plain view of prowling bluegills, while searching for food. We can, therefore, theoretically present the imitation in three ways: (1) a very slow bottom-crawling retrieve; (2) an appropriate mid-level retrieve; or (3) simply letting the neutrally buoyant fly slowly tumble toward the bottom.

Most dragonfly nymphs are capable of a short burst of speed; their ability to draw water into the anus and quickly expel it creates a sort of jet propulsion. If you slowly wade a clear, shallow, soft-bottomed pond, you will see little puffs of disturbed silt on the bottom ahead of you; these are the nymphs of burrowing species of dragonflies trying to get out of your way. Trout fishers, as Gary Borger points out, often retrieve a weighted nymph to imitate this "jetting" behavior, but we rarely enjoy such liberty in our cluttered, weed-infested waters. I have not observed this phenomenon except on the bottom. Such swimming nymphs are not a common occurrence in our ponds, and since bluegills seem to have an aversion to swimming flies of any kind, a slow, tumbling descent has proved to be the most productive way to present an Odonata nymph to warm-water fish. Moreover, a retrieve is very difficult in the weedy habi-

tat that these organisms prefer, and moving the fly slowly enough requires superhuman discipline.

This free-fall technique requires a fly that is only slightly heavier than neutral buoyancy; the slower the sink the better—an inch per second is optimum (see Tying with Neutral Buoyancy in Chapter 7). Mature bluegills tend to ignore a fast-sinking weighted nymph. The nymph will be most attractive to the fish as it slowly tumbles and free-falls through the weeds on its way to the bottom. The fish seem to enjoy descending with the offering and may circle it, examining it from every angle before taking the artificial. Although a smaller bluegill tends to snatch his prize and run (so the others can't take it away from him), larger fish sometimes will mouth the fly and quickly eject it with no lateral movement at all. As a consequence, strike detection may be dependent entirely on visibility. Any unnatural motion of the fly during this descent will spook the fish, but once it settles to the bottom or on vegetation, a slight lifting motion with the rod tip may induce a take, especially from smaller bluegills and juvenile bass. Big bluegills are generally turned off by fast movement of any sort. When the angler retrieves the nymph he has, in effect, converted it to a streamer, which mature bluegills may reject. It's not feasible to weedproof a nymph, and a retrieve will only result in constant snags. When skilled fly fishers finally begin to take these handsome, hard-fighting fellows seriously, they will be truly amazed at how discerning and intelligent they really are.

Tying nymphs with lead eyes (on top of the shank) or on the mini-jig heads available today, so the fly rides keel-style with the hook up, is helpful in brush and timber, but such patterns will still hang in the weeds and gather moss. Big bream invariably frequent the most densely vegetated areas of the pond, and depending upon the type of weeds present, heavily weighted flies are simply too snag prone. We need a very slow-sinking design. Moreover, while the prowling bluegill is attracted to subtle, natural movement, too much disturbance will spook him. A heavy sink-tip fly line and a large weedguard-equipped fly dragged through the weeds in a completely unnatural manner will send every mature bream in the area scurrying for the safety of the depths. The creatures that live in these weeds don't move plant stems and drag moss behind them. This type of commotion signifies the presence of an otter or diving bird, and the prudent angler will avoid such oafish behavior. Although imitating the swimming or jetting motion of Odonata nymphs is productive in some waters, attempts to impart that type of action to the fly in such tight habitat are usually counterproductive.

When fishing a nymph in the weeds, I use as short a line as possible. The closer I am to the "hole," the more control I have. Obviously, in weeds it is a lot easier to pick up 10 feet of line than 40 feet. Ease the tube or Kikk Boat right up to the weedbed and remain still—relax for a few minutes and watch the wildlife. These fish will spook at your approach, but will quickly recover and resume their normal activities. They are quite used to making hasty retreats from otters, cormorants, gar, bass, bowfin, and a variety of other predators. If the bluegills remained frightened for very long, they would starve to death. In this situation, you must fish slowly and quietly. Keep your feet still—those fins sound like a large predator—and avoid any sort of noise, including conversation with a companion in an adjacent weedbed. Keep the casts low and to a minimum. Use slide arm and bow-and-arrow casts, and lay the line and heavy butt sections of the leader on top of the weeds whenever possible. I sometimes overload the rod by two or three line-weights in order to cast a very short line and long leader. My chances of landing a big bream are also better with a short line. Few large fish will be brought to net through thirty feet or more of moss and weeds. In any case, many fish will be lost in this type of fishing. If the nymph is tied slightly heavier than neutral buoyancy, it will slowly tumble and fall in a lifelike manner, perhaps resting momentarily on a leaf or mat of vegetation. You won't be able to see the fly, so you'll have to look for indirect evidence of progress. If, after a period of time, a large amount of leader is still floating on the surface, the fly is resting on something, and a slight "jiggle" will recommence the tumbling action. Keep your attention riveted on the visible parts of the leader. A strike will be indicated by a sudden straightening of the leader. This is often quite subtle and demands the angler's undivided attention. This is another good reason for fishing a short line—those of us who are over fifty have trouble seeing these brief movements of the leader or line tip.

When the leader has disappeared below the surface, allow another minute or so to elapse. Bluegills sometimes will watch the nymph all the way to the bottom, even swimming along with it. A fish may not take the fly until it comes to rest. You may only have a few inches to retrieve the fly before it hangs in the weeds, but many strikes occur at this time. The nymph is now down in redear country, and I have taken some beautiful specimens of this handsome, hard-fighting, bottom-feeding bream on dragonfly nymphs resting right on the bottom below weedbeds. Depending upon the length of line you have out, you can sometimes impart further action with the rod tip by using a "lifting" motion, similar to the

Leisenring lift used by trout fishers to simulate an emerging nymph. Strikes also frequently occur the moment the fly hits the water, especially from small bass. If a big bass takes the nymph—they do on occasion—you're in real trouble in these dense weeds. Simply thank him for the memory, tie on a new tippet, and go on with your life!

The name of this game is patience. Each cast will take a couple of minutes—none of that fast cast and pick-up stuff. If I miss a fish, I usually go back to the same spot, but if I have had a hook-up or taken a fish, I usually move to a new location on the assumption (which may or may not be correct) that I have spooked all the fish in that area. Landing a one-pound bluegill through all that vegetation does, after all, create quite a disturbance. The angler should bear in mind, however, that these fish regain their composure quickly.

Strike indicators may be helpful, as long as you aren't fishing more than three feet deep. Also, be aware that casts often terminate with the indicator on target, but the errant fly may land on top of the adjacent weeds. Strikes commonly occur before the slow sinking nymph has straightened out the leader, and the fish may eject the fly with no movement of the indicator. These devices have a place in our arsenal, but they are not a panacea. I have always resisted strike indicators for aesthetic reasons. Since feeding bluegills are often too spooky to approach from the water, much of this fishing is done from the bank with bow and arrow and roll casts as well as plain old dapping. The little bobber makes me feel like a cane-pole bait-fisher. But strike indicators are indispensable in some situations, such as trying to suspend a sinking fly over the top of a brush pile or submerged weedbed, and for some anglers they may facilitate the use of slow-sinking nymphs. If you find those little fluorescent balls too "bobber-like" for your tastes, use a short piece of dry twig attached to the leader with a clove hitch. The twig is more natural and can be slipped off the clove hitch, leaving no knots in the leader. Another alternative is to use a small popping bug as an indicator. The problem with a dropper is a natural tendency to concentrate on the bug rather than nymph.

Colorado warm-water enthusiast Doug Tucker-Eccher has developed a new concept in indicators that enables the angler to fish vertically. He calls it a "flippin' leader." The level leader, of whatever length desired, runs through a little slip bobber, and a split shot is attached about eighteen inches above the fly. Therefore, there is never more than eighteen inches of leader below the indicator while casting. It is nearly impossible to cast a fixed indicator if it's more than a couple of feet above the fly, and Doug's system alleviates that problem. Once in the water, the split shot carries the fly down, through the bobber, until it reaches the bottom or is stopped by the fly-line connection knot. The fly can then be retrieved slowly a few inches off the bottom. This works better in the comparatively clean ponds of eastern Colorado, where Doug fishes, than in my cluttered waters, but I have used it successfully for redears and it has proved to be a deadly technique for channel catfish.

THE ELUSIVE REDEAR

The redear sunfish is really quite challenging. This fellow will test the mettle of the most seasoned cold-water nymph fisher. The redear stays near the bottom, searching for snails and other crustaceans, and will rarely rise to a dry. He behaves as recklessly as any sunfish while spawning, but at other times consistent success requires a sinking fly presented in his preferred feeding zone. I have been taking some nice redears recently on Jeff Hines' SS Damsel as it hovers enticingly near the bottom while suspended on an indicator.

The redear is every bit as gamy as his more popular cousin, the bluegill, and equals it in size. One-pounders are common in fertile habitat. Equipped with special grinding teeth in his throat, which are used to crush snails, he deserves the colloquial name "shellcracker." You don't have to use a snail pattern (though you'll find one in Borger's *Naturals*) because the redear is opportunistic and will readily take a nymph. Unlike bluegills, which normally cruise in groups, solitary individuals will frequently be observed patrolling the shallows. The redear ventures into open areas of the pond to feed, doesn't seem as cover-oriented as the bluegill, and rarely participates in insect emergences and other binge feeding activities. It is my impression that a large redear continually cruises the bottom, picking up tidbits of food here and there. I cannot associate this species with any particular habitat and have taken them in shallow, weedy areas as well as in the deepest parts of the pond.

The redear doesn't chase fast-swimming food forms. He is more inclined to graze than hunt and rarely responds to a rapidly retrieved nymph, streamer, or jig. The ideal presentation is a slow-moving offering on or very near the bottom. The nymph is most effective when suspended on a strike indicator at the appropriate depth. This is where Doug's flippin' leader really pays off.

STREAMERS

Streamers present fewer snag problems than do sparsely configured nymph patterns for three reasons: (1) you can tie them in a weed-resistant manner with mallard or pheasant flank feathers (an idea we owe to Chris Phillips, a superb Texas fly fisher); (2) some of the larger patterns will accommodate, though somewhat clumsily, a standard monofilament weedguard; and (3) streamers can be effectively fished along the edges of the weeds. When tied with just the right density, streamers can be worked over the top of a submerged weedbed rather than down in the vegetation itself. Big bluegills become voracious minnow feeders, as Tom Nixon used to point out in his popular warm-water seminars, but it has been my experience that baitfish imitations are less effective than insect patterns. It could well be that my limited success with bluegills in fishing the streamer is due to the fact that I never weight my streamers; I also fish them close to the surface or right in the surface film. In any case, I am normally targeting bass when I tie on a streamer.

Although shallow-water techniques are deadly for bass, a deeper-running baitfish imitation will take more bluegills. I don't recall ever seeing any species of bream chasing minnows on the surface the way bass and crappie occasionally do. Green sunfish, rock bass, and warmouth are minnow feeders to a much larger extent than are bluegills, and small streamers are very productive in ponds that have populations of these species. The redear sunfish, in my experience, does not feed on small fish at all. As a general rule of thumb, it is the sunfishes with larger mouths rather than those with smaller mouths that feed on minnows. Minnows and other baitfish are, of course, the prime forage for both white and black crappies.

Tiny jigs, weighted Woolly Buggers, and lead-eye flies such as Clouser's Minnow or Brooks Bouldin's Crappie Fly are all essentially baitfish imitations, and all consistently take bream. Those mini-jig heads that are so popular today come in three sizes—$1/64$ ounce, $1/80$ ounce, and $1/124$ ounce. The latter, tied in black or olive marabou, is absolutely deadly on bream, small bass, and, I've been told, on Arkansas trout as well. Some years ago, I was all excited about these lures and fished them regularly, but I was never really comfortable with the idea of using a jig. All it is, of course, is another heavily weighted fly, and there is no reason that it should offend one's sensibilities.

Jigs have become an indispensable tool in my bass fishing arsenal, but since I tend to categorize bream with trout, I'm reluctant to use lures of any kind in their pursuit. My willingness to use a lure on my fly rod has increased as I've gained understanding of the black bass and his habitat, but I prefer to use flies only with bluegills. All these fast-sinking flies and lures can only be fished in relatively open water for obvious reasons.

The success of the $\frac{1}{124}$-ounce jig, which is on a size 12 hook, did lead to one valuable conclusion: bream streamers must be very small. Bream do not seem inclined to chase larger baitfish, even two-inch minnows, but do feed on the tiny fry of many species. Catfish and bullhead fry are especially vulnerable to bream predation, due to their tight schooling behavior, and big bream will gather around one of these ball-shaped schools and pig out. Normally, this activity occurs in shallow water and can be observed from the bank. If the angler can place a small black streamer or wet fly into the melee without spooking the fish, his skill will be amply rewarded. Green sunfish and warmouth are especially inclined to attack schools of fry (one reason they are never stocked in managed ponds) and such behavior is, unfortunately, part of the crappie's daily routine. Bass also feed on schooling fry in the same manner, but they are very opportunistic and more inclined to accept a larger, noisily presented fly. Generally speaking, bass require less delicacy and finesse and are more easily fooled than mature bluegills.

One interesting application for heavily weighted flies and mini-jigs is what I call "tube trolling." Whenever I cross an expanse of open water in the tube or Kikk boat, I tie on a $\frac{1}{64}$-ounce jig or weighted Woolly Bugger, normally red and white. I stay with the floating line unless I am crossing very deep water. I play out fifty or sixty feet of line and troll the jig deep as I kick across the pond or along the dropoff on larger lakes. This makes the trip back to the car less tedious, and I have caught some really huge catfish and bass in this admittedly churlish manner. This is also an effective method to locate a deep school of white crappies. They are not much of a game fish, but they sure taste good rolled in cornmeal and fried over a campfire. (Obviously, my veneration of the trout-like bluegill does not extend to crappies and catfish; I put them in the same class as chub or whitefish. Catfish are often taken while trolling the jig and meet the same fate. Incidentally, this is the only workable method that I have found to consistently take channel cats on the fly rod—short of bait, that is.)

Streamers are a fundamental part of any bass fisher's arsenal. I have two favorites—the standard Marabou Muddler in various sizes and colors and my own Fathead Diver (see Chapter 7). These are both shallow-running patterns. I use the diver in size 8 or 10, in weedy habitats and the muddler in open water. During major emergences of aquatic and certain terrestrial insects, these are the flies of choice to simulate the myriad baitfishes and juvenile sunfish that are drawn out of the cover to feed on the hatch. While thus addressing the secondary aspects of such hatches, big bream will sometimes take the streamer while ignoring a small dry. Although presenting a hatch-matching dry fly to the insect feeders is great fun, a baitfish imitation will take larger bream as well as bass during these feeding frenzies. The bream do not chase the baitfish to the surface as bass do, and a weighted streamer or mini-jig may be required to reach the big bluegill (as discussed in Chapter 3). Such occurrences notwithstanding, small fish are much less significant than are insects and crustaceans in the bream's diet. The Marabou Muddler is unbeatable on schooling bass. I tie the pattern in a variety of colors, usually on size 8. The deer-hair head can be trimmed to achieve neutral buoyancy, so the fly just barely sinks, thereby gaining the advantage of a submerged offering without the snag problems of a full-sinking fly. Since few organisms float on top of the water, learning to tie with neutral buoyancy is a crucial aspect of warm-water fly fishing. Have you ever seen a frog, snake, baby gator, or turtle floating on its belly with its body high and dry? Most terrestrial insects, such as large beetles, also tend to sink down in the surface film when they fall in the pond.

Although I prefer the Marabou Muddler design, other anglers use the Whitlock "match-the-minnow" series very successfully. My good friend and expert angler, Brooks Bouldin, of Houston, swears by the Zonker flies. Others, such as East Texas angler Royce Feaster, tie their streamers in the Matuka style. I cannot, however, achieve the desired neutral buoyancy with any of those designs; they all sink too fast for my taste.

SINKING WORMS—WOOLLY AND OTHERWISE

Every southern country boy knows that a creekside catalpa tree means red hot "brim" fishing in August when the black-and-yellow striped " 'tawba" worms reach maturity and drop from the host branches to complete their life cycle. Those unfortunate worms who have spent their childhood on a limb that overhangs the creek will end their life in the gut of a big bluegill. The boy also knows that the very best bream bait is either the larvae of the red wasp or the grub-like larvae of certain large beetles. He intuitively realizes that wasp and beetle larvae don't fall in the water; in using these baits he is actually representing the worms and caterpillars that thrive in the deciduous trees along the creek. He would use the worms themselves if he could, but they are soft and mushy and won't stay on the hook unless he puts them in cornmeal and keeps them cool for a couple of days. The grubs and wasp larvae can be used immediately. (Please don't ask how I know all of this!)

There are dozens, perhaps hundreds, of species of arboreal Lepidoptera that dwell in the hardwood forests that line southern creeks and ponds. They come in all sizes and colors. Some are "hackled," but most are smooth and sink rather quickly when they land on the water. Few ever make it to the bottom! When the worms drop from the host tree it is not an accident, as many anglers assume, but part of the moth's life cycle. When the larvae reach a certain stage of maturity, they either fall or, in the case of some species, lower themselves to the ground on a gossamer strand of silk, where they over-winter and pupate to emerge the following year as an adult moth. In the Deep South, some species may have more than one annual generation.

The observant angler will be aware of such phenomena on his home water and will learn which worms will be present on each species of tree as the season progresses. Most of these insects are "host specific" and will only be found on certain types of trees. (For example, the catalpa sphinx moth lays eggs *only* on catalpa trees.) Through study and observation, the warm-water fly fisher will know when to expect these events. The drops usually occur within a short period, but the bream will stay in the area for several days thereafter—hoping, I suppose, that more worms will be forthcoming. Any time overhanging branches show signs of recent insect damage, a slow sinking Woolly Worm is called for. Since I am on the pond nearly every day and can watch the maturation process of the worms, I also can be on the spot when the drop occurs. I have never understood how the bream know a drop is imminent, but believe it or not they gather under the tree before the caterpillars actually start falling.

It would be ludicrous for me to suggest that one must match the color and size of each larvae in tying Woolly Worms. It is important, however, to imitate the slow-sinking motion of the organism, and I do believe that the size and basic coloration of the fly could be a factor in attracting the larger, more discerning adult fish. At any rate, attempting to duplicate actual organisms is what makes fly tying so much fun. When I am at my vise in the middle of December, I may be tying an imitation of a worm that I know will be on a specific limb of a certain oak tree in the second week of August. Observation and study is a fundamental part of the fly-fishing experience.

One way to ascertain the presence of Lepidoptera larvae, which are sometimes high in the host tree, is to look for droppings on the ground. As every vegetable gardener knows, these worms defecate constantly; the telltale droppings signify trouble on the tomato plant, and the gardener then looks for the hornworms themselves. I use the same tech-

A sinking Woolly Worm should be fished with no retrieve.

Woolly Worm

nique while walking through the woods toward the pond or creek. Large numbers of tiny pellets under the hickory trees, for example, tell me to try a Woolly Worm under overhanging branches of that species of tree. I also know from experience and observation that in late summer hickory worms will be black with two orange stripes on each side. They will be bristled, calling for a size 6 imitation with clipped hackle. A great deal of interesting and useful information can be acquired through careful observation.

If exact imitation is not crucial for success, the behavior of the fly is. I recently fished a drop of small, green oakworms with a friend. The larvae were falling in considerable numbers and the bream were feeding on them as they sank slowly toward the bottom. We were both using the same pattern, an appropriate Woolly Worm, but my friend was not taking fish. Once I reminded him that worms are not equipped with any anatomical appendages to propel themselves through the water, he stopped retrieving the fly like a streamer and began taking the handsome eight- to nine-inch bluegills.

Most of these larvae are either smooth or bristled. Only a few have long "hackle." I still tie all my Woolly Worms with a full palmered hackle, though, and trim it off accordingly while I am fishing. I rarely add weight, since I want a very slow sink rate. Instead I adjust the amount of dressing and hook style to achieve the desired density.

DREDGING THE BOTTOM

Although I find nymph fishing with a floating line tolerably enjoyable, I confess that full sinking lines are an absolute act of desperation. Nevertheless, the technique is deadly in waters where the cover situation permits its use. And to be quite frank, sinking lines are the only way to take larger bass on flies consistently. This is slow fishing; it's hard work that requires a great deal of patience and persistence. I rarely fish deep in pond habitat, though it is the best way to approach the local lunk-

Strike detection is nearly impossible with a heavy sinking line.

ers. My failure to do so is partly a matter of laziness and obstinacy, but it's also true that the cover is too tight in many southern ponds to effectively use sinking lines. In a large impoundment, however, such lines are a necessity. The angler who fishes only topwater will spend most of his time futilely casting to fish that aren't there. The future of fly rodding for bass is contingent upon the development of bottom-crawling techniques. A few of us fly fishers may be willing to cast topwater flies all day to empty water, but sane people want to catch fish.

Dave McMillan, of Fort Worth, has mastered the sinking line; he has taken more trophy bass from pond waters than any fly fisher I know. He uses a full-sinking line with floating flies and adjusts the length of the leader to achieve the desired fishing depth. The line, of course, lies on the bottom, but the floating fly rides just above vegetation and debris. Dave's system demands extraordinary skill and patience; to call it "challenging" is an understatement. He has proved that it can be done, though at times I find it a little *too* challenging. He fishes this rig *very, very* slowly. Dave says he smokes an entire cigarette before beginning the retrieve. Although as unhealthy for him as for the bass, the method has accounted for farm-pond lunkers up to twelve pounds! His most productive pattern is a mean-looking creation tied with a concave deer hair head and long (8- to 10-inch) saddle hackles. Admittedly, this and similar deep-water fly-fishing systems are not for everyone, but several dedicated fly fishers who persist in doing it the hard way consistently take lethargic, subsurface bass.

Bill Lambing, of Lufkin, Texas, makes a credible showing with a small jig and a long leader on a floating line. I frequently use Bill's system; it's effective when the fish are moving around a little but not when they are inactive. Brian Camp, of Forth Worth, fishes a weighted all-rabbit-strip pattern flat on the bottom, just as if it were a plastic worm. Brian reports that the bass will hang on to this fly long enough for him to detect the pick-up. Strike detection is the number one problem here—with thirty feet or more of heavy line lying on the muddy bottom, the angler simply cannot feel the subtle take. The bass will suck in the fly, along with a mouthful of water; if it doesn't feel a life-like object in his mouth, the fish will rapidly eject it. I have personally observed bass in a clear pond repeatedly taking and ejecting a bottom-crawling fly without the angler ever realiz-

ing that he had a strike. Brian and Dave have developed the ability to feel that faint tap or slight resistance and react accordingly. I don't know how they do it. I think they are gifted with some kind of extrasensory perception.

Feeling the strike is only part of the problem. Hooking the fish is nearly as difficult. Driving the hook into the hard jaw of a bass requires the use of the Whitlock straight-line technique. Those of us who carry trout-fishing baggage instinctively raise the rod tip on a strike. But it is very hard to hook a bass that way; you must use the line hand and rod butt as Dave demonstrates in his clinics. I have taught the method to a number of novices in our Texas clinics who have long since mastered it, but I still struggle to stop raising the rod in what Jimmy Nix calls the "Orvis strike," after their famous logo. Old habits are hard to break.

Whitlock's technique requires a straight line but that may be impossible in deeper water. If I cast a comfortable distance in fifteen feet of water, my retrieve begins with a substantial angle on the line. Halfway through the retrieve the rod tip is way under the water, perhaps forty-five degrees to the surface, in order to maintain the straight line. In the final twenty feet, where most strikes occur (at least where those that I can *feel* occur), the fly line is virtually perpendicular and striking with my stripping hand is clearly impossible. I feel very foolish in this comical circumstance, jerking on the rod tip in utter futility in a vain attempt to set the hook. I suspect that many times the bass has a hold of the rabbit-strip tail and the hook is never in his mouth. To make matters worse, the fish invariably swims toward you. I can stick an occasional fish, but the enjoyment isn't there—it becomes work!

I have always believed that if only I could tie just the right fly I could keep up with the plastic-worm casters. But the texture of a fly simply can't compete with the texture of those soft-plastic baits; they feel so realistic that the fish rarely detects the fraud. Many times a bass will actually swallow a soft-plastic lure even if the angler reacts too slowly. (For this reason, plastic salmon eggs and worms have been defined as "bait" in some states and are not permitted on trout streams restricted to artificials.) Soft plastic is akin to live bait, and strike detection is never a problem in any kind of bait fishing. Those of us who started our angling careers catching trout on garden worms had a rude awakening when we graduated to weighted nymphs; we had to retune all our senses to detect the strike. Deep-water bass fishing is even more difficult than nymphing for trout because it is virtually impossible, at least for those of us without ESP, to feel the normally subtle pick-up through that heavy line, especially with the necessarily slow retrieve and continual false strikes that occur as the fly tumbles through submerged timber, weeds, and moss. This is why worm casters outfish us so badly. My observations have confirmed that our flies actually have more visual fish appeal than do the worms.

We experienced a severe drought in East Texas several summers ago and the local pond was very low and crystal clear. One morning I was casting a weighted Hare Water Pup on a sink-tip line without success as a neighborhood girl watched from her perch high in a pondside oak tree. Suddenly she shouted, "You need to sharpen your hook, Mr. Ellis, you're getting lots of bites." The following morning, I sent her back up the tree with a pencil, pad, and instructions to record her observations. She could see the small, hungry bass repeatedly picking up and ejecting my fly while I felt nothing. I switched to a four-inch plastic worm tied on an eight-weight fly line. This time, the bass picked up the worm and swam away with it; I could even see the fly line moving as the fish actually swallowed the bait. My young assistant indicated that the fish seemed to "go for" the flies more than the worm, but "spit them out" too fast. I found it interesting that while this eleven-year-old could grasp my desire to catch fish on the flies I had tied, her bass-fishing father found the whole thing incomprehensible. "Why not just use the worm?" he asked. Good question. (My research assistant has now become a charming young woman who shows little interest in climbing trees and watching fish.)

A four-inch plastic worm will cast easily on an eight-weight fly line. Strike detection is no problem, and this best-of-all bass baits fishes even better when unencumbered by lead weight. Despite the obvious aesthetic objections and the fact that it's definitely a "cop-out," it fishes incredibly well on the fly rod and it's lots of fun. When I wrote the first edition of this work, I strongly discouraged the use of soft plastics on the fly rod because I had experienced too many problems with deeply hooked fish. At that time my reaction time was so slow (because the heavy, full-sinking line absorbed the subtle strike) that the fish sometimes swallowed the worm before I could strike. I restricted its use to the casting rod because the light monofilament line provided a more direct connection to the bait so that even the slightest movement was immediately transferred to the rod tip. I have since solved the problem by using lighter lines. A slow sinking USL line, a standard weight-forward intermediate, a sink-tip, or even a floating line with a longer leader all work fine—in fact, any line with a sink rate below about two-and-a-half inches per second will do the job. I have also discovered that I can crimp the barb without the bait flying off the hook while casting. Now I use barbless hooks all the time for deep bass in large lakes, and nearly all my fish are hooked in the lip or mouth. I shudder to think what Brian or Dave could do with *this* thing if they should ever, God forbid, sink to that level—they just might drive a dedicated casting rod fisherman to the edge of suicide!

Although I have fallen from the exalted assemblage of "flies only" brethren, I have learned something about fishing bass flies on heavy lines that is worth sharing here. Deep fishing will never be a piece of cake, but at least it's possible, in part due to the new Uniform Sinking Lines from Scientific Anglers. The weight is distributed in such a way that the line sinks as a unit, giving the angler a fairly straight connection to the fly. The old-style lines were heavier in the belly section, which made strike detection nearly impossible. But the USL design eliminates sag. These lines are available in five sink rates—the Wet Cel I is very slow (ideal for the four-inch worm) and the Wet Cel V sinks like a rock.

I can offer a few hard-learned lessons in using these lines in bass waters. First, use the slowest sink rate possible in a given situation; the faster lines will sink deeper into the mud, aggravating strike detection problems. In eight to ten feet of water, for example, the three-inch-per second rate of the Wet Cel III is adequate to put the fly on the bottom in a half minute. Second, whenever possible, try to work only the edges rather than the middle of weedbeds and other heavy cover. False strikes, as the weedguard-equipped fly temporarily hangs up on weeds and debris, only compound your problems. Also, our flies are not as weedproof as the plastic worm and they tend to gather moss on the head. But since bass are often found below the weeds, you may have no choice. Third, you may find it necessary to retrieve the fly faster than you would prefer. Ideally, since these bottom-crawling offerings represent slow-moving amphibians, they should be retrieved very slowly. The slower the retrieve, though, the less likely you will feel the pick-up. The rule is to retrieve as fast as you can get away with; if you're not getting strikes, slow down. It's all trial and error. Fourth, avoid weighted flies. Tie with neutral buoyancy and let the line take the fly down, adjusting leader length accordingly. This is especially true in cluttered southern lakes where a weighted fly will gather moss, pine needles, and bits of decaying wood on every retrieve. The weedguard may prevent an actual snag, but debris still gathers around the head of the fly. The plastic worm is totally smooth with no protrusions, and our fly designs should, as far as possible, imitate that feature. Protruding lead eyes, for example, won't work in such waters, but bass are surely attracted to something that stirs up mud and silt. Bass fishermen tell me that on a Carolina-rig (in which the sinker is pegged above the bait), at least one strike in three is on the sinker rather than the worm. Finally, keep a worm-rigged casting rod in the boat; it not only can locate fish, but it will serve as a vital "control" in your experimentation. If you know the fish are there, you will be motivated to continue your fly fishing efforts.

Bream are easier to take than bass on deeply fished flies because they take the fly much more forcefully. A bluegill tries to swim away with an item of food before he eats it, whereas the bass may not move laterally at all. Juvenile bluegills are competitive with each other—they fight over food—but young bass do not seem to learn that behavior to any extent. The bluegill will also drop the fly, but he gives you a detectable strike first. You can feel bluegills ganging up on the plastic worm, trying to carry it off, as you retrieve it. It's an entirely different kind of take.

The warm-water angler strikes a bass with the line hand and rod butt.

The reader may opt to avoid this type of fishing entirely. I did for many years; if there was no surface action, I simply, as we say in Texas, went "to the house." I still prefer an evening mosquito hatch on a tranquil pond, but there are too many bass being taken from our big lakes to continue ignoring the fishery. We have the delivery system with the USL lines, but we still have a long way to go on fly patterns. I am convinced that deep bass fishing with flies will never have wide appeal until patterns are developed with a soft, rubbery texture. Meanwhile, we must learn how to find fish in big water, and avail ourselves of the options available.

6

THE BASS OR
BREAM DILEMMA

The afternoon sun has just slipped behind the tall pines that line the west bank of the pond. Dozens of rings ripple the surface as bream rise to hatching mosquitoes. I quickly assemble my three-weight Sage, tie a small grizzly-hackled dry to the fine tippet, and quietly ease the float tube into the warm water. I work out a few feet of line; the fly lands lightly on the slick surface and instantly disappears in a swirl. A husky Texas bluegill strains the little rod as he bores toward the bottom. Returning the scrappy fellow to the dark water, I savor the moment—the beauty of the woods reflected on the pond's surface, the delight of a nice fish on a fine rod, and the euphoria of satisfying contentment that all fly fishers know so well.

Suddenly my reverie is shattered by a noisy splash along the bank behind me. A dozen tiny minnows clear the water together, a fast-moving wake in hot pursuit. The water boils and half the school disappears in the maw of a monster bass. My instincts in command, I irrationally cast the mangled little dry to the feeding fish. I am secretly relieved when it's ignored. I curse myself, as I have done a dozen times before, for choosing this little three-weight. Opportunities like this only arise occasionally, however, and that little Sage is so much more enjoyable for bream fishing. The minnows jump again. My eight-weight and box of bass flies are in the pickup. By the time I kick to the bank, get out of the tube, walk to the truck, assemble the outfit, and return to the fishing, the feeding activity will be over, and I'll be stuck with that "meat stick" the rest of the evening.

The big fish comes out of the water, crashing down on the hapless minnows. "Still within casting range," I mutter aloud, fumbling through the box of small dries and nymphs. Then I notice a bedraggled old Dahlberg that's been on the drying patch of the tube all summer. Logic yields to raw emotion, and with a total disregard for the laws of physics, I bite off the tippet, tie the diver to the butt section, and flail the air frantically trying to force the light line to push this powder puff to the still-feeding bass. Fly, leader, and line fall in a hopeless pile in front of the tube. The fish will finish his supper in peace. I take a pinch of snuff, scan the bank to see if anyone was watching, and try to regain my composure.

Most warm-water fly fishers, at least light-tackle enthusiasts, have suffered a similar experience, agonizing over tackle selection on every outing thereafter. The obvious answer, of course, is to take two rods. But if the spare isn't rigged and ready it doesn't help you very much, and one soon tires of dragging it around. Certain small craft, such as Brooks Bouldin's Kikk boat, are designed to carry an extra rod and there's no problem in doing so when fishing from a jon boat or other large craft. Much pond and creek fishing is done, however, from a tube or wading or walking the bank. Carrying an extra rod is, at best, awkward. In actual practice, one rarely switches rods while fishing, and the two-rod solution soon becomes burdensome. Moreover, the spare outfit is in real danger of being forgotten somewhere, dropped overboard, or broken.

I have gone through a number of phases in my approach to this problem. I carried a spare for a while. At one time I swore off light tackle and used an eight-weight exclusively, but I was depriving myself of the fun of bream fishing. Then I tried the "six-weight" compromise; the tackle was too heavy for enjoyable bream fishing, too light for effective bass fishing. Every warm-water angler must find his own solution to this; some are strictly bass-oriented, especially those that we have managed to convert from the casting rod. They prefer to cast huge flies to big fish in large impoundments. They don't own a light outfit, tend to sneer at bream and small bass, and rarely fish farm ponds. Other southern fly fishers are exclusively panfish-oriented and find no need for heavy gear. The well-equipped, versatile southern angler should have three outfits: a lightweight trout rod for panfishing, a heavy outfit for serious bass fishing, and something in between for special situations. A three-weight, a six-weight, and a nine-weight is a good combination.

I rarely use anything heavier than a four- or five-weight outfit any-more and have learned to accept the occasional lost fish or missed op-portunity. I'm not on a macho trip and not terribly concerned about catching trophy fish. The vast majority of farm-pond bass are under two pounds anyway. I can handle a pretty good fish on my four- or five-weight Loomis, if the cover situation isn't too bad, and size 6 streamers, divers, and bugs are castable and quite adequate to entice feeding bass. I do use a heavy tippet, usually 2X, on small bass flies. Remember that a bass has sandpaper-like teeth. If he's hooked inside the mouth, the leader will be badly frayed. I have lost many nice bass because I was too lazy to retie the fly after each fish.

My favorite rod is my Sage 389LL. This little springcreek rod is a pure joy to cast and will handle sparsely tied flies up to a size 8. A bulky size 8, such as a mini-bug or hopper, is, admittedly, pushing its limit, but I have taken hundreds of school bass, which run one to three pounds, on this rod—nearly all on size 8 Marabou Muddlers and size 10 Fathead Divers with 4X tippets. The three-weight is perfect, of course, for dry-fly and nymph fishing for bream. I must also confess that I have lost a lot of wallhangers on this tackle, and the angler who cannot accept that shouldn't fish warm waters with trout gear. Because of the inevitability of lost fish, the light-tackle enthusiast should always crimp his barbs and avoid stainless hooks.

My six-weight Sage is a beautiful rod that handles anything up to a size 2 hair bug (size 2 sproat, not stinger). It is too heavy for bream and too light for bass, but it's a good compromise rod—and I usually take it to new waters when I don't know what to expect. I use it a lot in the very early spring on spawning bass and in the swamp where I need just a little more muscle to horse fish out of the moss. It's also my rod of choice for deep-water crappie fishing. It will cast the heavily weighted flies required while still providing a little fun from the crap-pie. I can cast a prettier line on this rod than any tackle I have and I always choose it when I am trying to "look good" (e.g., a casting clinic).

When I go to a big lake for serious bass fishing, I leave all the light gear at home. I have two very stiff, powerful Diamondback rods made by The Diamondback Company of Stowe, Vermont. These are real meat sticks and have the backbone to work big bass out of heavy cover or subdue an angry bowfin in a maze of cypress roots. L.L. Bean used to handle them, and it is the rod Dave Whitlock uses on his famous "Fly Fishing For Bass" video. I bought the eight-weight first, but it wouldn't quite handle the very largest, heaviest flies that I needed on

East Texas impoundments. By that time, L.L. Bean had switched to another manufacturer, so I called Diamondback directly and they built me a fine ten-weight rod! I use that big stick when I go to Sam Rayburn or Toledo Bend with one of my boat-fishing, trophy-oriented friends. To be brutally frank, after an hour of casting that heavy tackle, I'm usually ready to go home (unless they're biting, of course). That type of fishing, along with an occasional trip to the saltwater flats, is a nice change of pace, but my heart is in light-tackle fishing on farm ponds, creeks, and swamps.

TUBES, BOATS, AND OTHER WATERCRAFT

Since most of our fishing is done in still water, soft-bottomed ponds, and lakes, flotation devices are crucial. My float tube is my constant companion. It stays in the back of my pickup and I use it nearly every day. A quality float tube is an absolute necessity for the warm-water fly fisher but it's not the total answer. You can't use a tube in weedbeds, in fallen timber, or wherever submerged cover is less than a couple of feet deep. In such areas, you'll need some sort of shallow draft craft. Jon

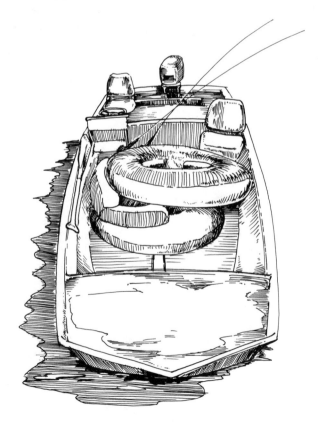

boats and canoes are fine if you have someone to paddle for you, but if you're alone the slightest breeze will blow the boat all over the pond—and you won't be able to paddle and fish at the same time.

The most versatile fly-fishing craft I know is the Kikk boat, manufactured by Brooks Bouldin of The Angler's Edge in Houston, Texas. Although heavier than a float tube, one man can carry it for a short distance. When the pontoons are well inflated it draws virtually no water and you can slide over weeds, logs—anything. You can propel it with swim fins or with a paddle in shallow situations. I use the swim fins to maneuver while fishing and when I want to move some distance, I simply put my feet up on the pontoons and use the paddle. Best of all, Velcro straps provide safe storage for an extra rod. Since you are well out of the water, casting is much easier. (Incidentally, it is less of a problem to answer the call of nature—depending upon one's gender.) Any fly fisher should avoid drinking beer at lunch if he/she is going to be float tubing in the afternoon! The Kikk boat is convenient to transport when deflated, but it's too heavy to carry long distances. My stalwart friend Ross Wilhite did carry his Kikk boat on his back for ten miles into a Wyoming lake; just a matter of motivation, I guess.

The main advantage of the tube is its convenience. I can grab it out of the back of the pickup, throw it over a barbed-wire fence, and carry it with one hand to the lake. All my gear is in the side pockets, waders are in the back pocket, and the fins are strapped to the tube with a belt. I can easily carry everything I need in one trip. I do recommend high-quality, graphite scuba fins. Believe me, when it's nearly dark and you're a half-mile from the car, tired and eager for happy hour, you'll be glad you spent the extra money so you won't be all night getting back. Some years ago, I bought a pair of hinged devices that strap on the ankles. They allow one to move forward instead of only backward. They worked great while fishing, but when night fell a moderate breeze prevented my making any headway. I finally got out on the bank and had a horrible struggle through dense thickets. It was a real nightmare, and those things went up on a shelf where they remain to this day!

Much has been written on tubing techniques. I will not reiterate, but I would like to offer one valuable tip. If you're right-handed, keep the bank that you are casting toward on your left. This is your most comfortable and natural casting position. From where you are seated at this moment, put down the book and pretend the bank is on your left and that you are casting toward it. Now pretend it's on your right. See what I mean? If you are left-handed, it's just the opposite. Simply put, the right-handed tuber moves around the pond in a counterclockwise direction.

The same principle applies to other situations as well. Suppose you are preparing to fish a tailwater river on slack water. You are seated in the bow of a canoe, facing forward. Your guide is paddling in the back. The plan is to work upstream until they start generating and come back down with the current. As a right-handed caster, you will be most comfortable fishing up the left bank, looking upstream. The other bank will be on your left on the return trip. (Other things being equal, of course. If the fish are all along the right bank, you have no choice in the matter.)

Finally, if you plan to purchase a power boat for fishing the big lakes, look for a boat that's free of cleats, latches, and other protrusions that can catch your shooting line. I use a seventeen-foot Alumacraft with a thirty-horse Mariner motor. This boat is really spartan; there is nothing to get in the way. I have a bow deck devoid of hardware that serves as a casting platform. The only place your fly line could get caught on my boat is on the motor itself, and I have a net to throw over it to prevent that possibility. There is nothing worse than trying to fly fish from a boat with a lot of junk to hang up your line! A transom-mounted trolling motor doesn't work as well as a bow mount, but at least it's out of the way. When you go shopping for your boat, take the float tube dimensions with you and make sure you can conveniently carry two tubes—one upside down on the other. You and your fishing companion will probably wish to carry them in the boat from time to time. Since it lies flat deflated, the Kikk boat is excellent for boat transportation. It's also heavy enough not to blow away when the boat is running, and it inflates in minutes with a twelve-volt pump supplied by the manufacturer. The fly fisher is well-advised to stay away from those elaborately painted, high-powered bass boats with their seats, consoles, live wells, chrome hardware, bow-mounted trolling motor, etc. We need a large, open boat.

Handling any sort of boat in the wind is nearly impossible while fly fishing. When I am alone, I find that I have to anchor the boat in order to fish. When there are two of us in the boat, we simply take turns fishing and operating the electric trolling motor. Many bass fishermen use foot-controlled trolling motors, but that pedal looks like the worst kind of line-hanger and I haven't invested in one. If there are two anglers fly fishing from a boat at the same time, observe the following rule to avoid tangles: Do not pick up to cast unless your companion's line is on the water. Although a power boat of some kind is a virtual necessity for the

The author uses his boat for transportation, but prefers to fish from the tube.

serious warm-water enthusiast, fishing from it is a last resort and it is much better to carry a personal watercraft in your boat and fish from it instead. If you moor the boat in open water and intend to be some distance from it, leave a large note indicating that you are all right. Other boaters may think you have fallen overboard and needlessly alert the authorities. We are starting to get restrictions prohibiting float tubes on some public waters. This is a disturbing trend, and if we have accidents, or if the authorities get complaints, we may lose our tubing privileges on public lakes.

Speaking of accidents, the inner tube will deteriorate when frequently exposed to the water. It should be replaced every season. The back rest tube, which stays dry, may last for years, but the main tube dry rots in a few months. No tire tube is designed for use in water, but I find that a twenty-inch *radial* truck tube lasts the whole season. If I buy the cheaper, thinner *bias* tube, it may not even last through the summer. If the inner tube deflates between outings, I throw it away immediately and put in a new one. Don't try to patch or stretch the life of these tubes; they're not that expensive and your life is quite literally at risk. The nylon bag lasts forever. I have a Buck's Bag more than ten years old. It has been used thousands of times, left out in the sun, and abused in every imaginable way, but it's still serviceable.

THE BREAM-FISHER'S VEST

The warm-water fly fisher carries the same sundry items as a trout fisher with a few exceptions. A first-aid kit with instructions from your doctor on the field treatment of snake bite (they all have different opinions) should be included. The warm-water angler may also find himself stuck in the woods overnight, and some waterproof matches, a rain poncho, and water purification tablets are a good idea. One perspires heavily in this hot, humid climate, so drinking water must always be available. Carry some in the car, the boat, and the tube pocket. Most anglers carry insect repellent. It's a must in the southern fisheries.

There are many ways that an angler can get stranded. Sudden water releases from downstream dams can leave you with no navigable egress from a backwater swamp. Dangerous thunderstorms can prevent your crossing a large lake before nightfall or a twilight mosquito hatch on the creek bottom may tempt you to throw caution to the wind and stay with the rise. Unless you have a dependable outboard motor, never fish downstream from your car in any southern tailwater river. The Corps of Engineers may open those gates at any time—published generating schedules notwithstanding—and you may not be able to make your way back on the bank because of the vegetation. Only a local expert, equipped with a light, can negotiate the southern woods at night. Bear in mind that alligators and venomous snakes, although shy and reclusive by day, become much more aggressive under the cover of darkness. I know fly fishers who carry a small-caliber revolver in their vest, but I don't recommend the practice.

Neoprene waders are too hot; lightweight nylon is more fragile, but the comfort is worth the compromise. I carry a patch of material from old waders and a tube of Goop. It takes only a few minutes to make a repair. Because of the abundance of thorny plants in these areas, it's best to take your waders off when walking through wooded areas. My nylon, stocking-foot Rangers fold small enough to put in the big pocket on the back of my vest. I have an old pair of cheap canvas wading shoes that I use when wading and a pair of neoprene booties that protect the wader feet while tubing. Also, watch for thorns when carrying the tube. Bill Lambing, president of Pineywoods Fly Fishers, once failed to do so and his tube deflated shortly after launching. Had it not been for the secondary backrest tube, he would have been in serious trouble!

The new lightweight mesh vests are ideal for our fishing. Make sure to buy the shortest "shorty" you can find, otherwise, fly boxes will get water in them while tubing. This is one item you should not buy from a cat-alog—the vest must fit properly. I recently purchased a very expensive Patagonia vest designed for the flats fisherman. This is the best investment I ever made. It's a wonderful vest and would be a bargain at twice the money. How I regret the years I spent in a cheap, uncomfortable, ill-fitting vest, drying out my fly boxes after every outing. Don't scrimp on the vest—get a good one.

FLY LINES

There are lines available today for every conceivable angling applica-tion. As a consequence, line selection is very confusing to the new warm-water enthusiast. The single most important development in re-cent years, however, is the new Uniform Sinking Lines from Scientific Anglers. Available in five weights, these lines are slightly heavier in the tip section and sink as a unit without the horrible belly sag of the old lines. As we discussed in Chapter 5, this technology makes deep-water bass fishing possible.

I rarely use bass bug taper lines. Unless you are going to cast really enormous bugs, the short heavy head will do you more harm than good. They are too noisy when presented, impossible to roll cast, and if you tie on a small fly they will roll over in a sort of reverse tailing loop. I prefer the standard weight-forward line with a thirty-foot head. There's no problem handling a 2/0 bug on a regular WF8F line. Beware of longer heads, however. I once bought an English-made nine-weight line and found that I couldn't cast the bug. Did you ever inadvertently miss a guide while stringing the rod and wonder why you were casting so horribly? That's the way I felt—it was very frustrating. Finally, I discov-ered that the line had a forty-foot head instead of our standard thirty, and that made all the difference in the world! The line went up on a shelf where it remains today.

I have learned to buy only the best line the manufacturer offers; it's more than worth the extra ten bucks. I have several Cortland lines and a couple of very fine lines from L.L. Bean, but I lean toward Scientific Anglers. I didn't like their Air-Cel Supreme series, but the new Ultra is great, and they have the widest selection of special-purpose lines on the market. My first serious fly fishing was with the original Air-Cel in 1961, and it was such an improvement over the sticky, oiled lines that I remembered as a child that I will always be an "Air-Cel man." Manu-facturers claim that their new lines gradually emit a lubricating substance of some sort and that they should not be dressed. In my experience, they still dry out and require the application of a dressing for casting ease. Although the manufacturers may not approve, I advise applying copious amounts of Armor-All vinyl cleaner to the line. I have been using the product for five years and I am getting several times the service from my lines. I fish over 200 days a year and I used to buy new lines annually. Since I started using Armor-All, my lines are lasting for three or four years. They stay nice and flexible all the time, I have no more cracking problems, and a line can stay on the spool for months yet come off as supple as the day it was new. I spray the Armor-All right on the reel spool and turn the reel to saturate the whole line. I do this before I fish and again when I put the reel away. I have had no problem with the product gumming-up reel gears or anything like that. I really believe those expensive little applicator bottles of line dressing are filled with Armor-All or something very similar!

I attended a Lefty Kreh seminar some years ago and was horrified when he pointed out that fluorescent lights will break down the PVC coating on fly lines. I had those lights in my tying room with lines and reels scattered about in the open! I put a stop to that as soon as I got home, and that may be another reason my lines are lasting longer. They should not be stored in the sun either. I have a friend who carries a fly rod on the gun rack of his pickup. He wonders why his line is always stiff and cracked! Warm-water and saltwater anglers often find themselves in boats with gasoline motors; they should strive to keep the fly line away from the motor area. Any petroleum product will devastate a fly line. I was once casting to small ladyfish in a Louisiana canal with a brand-new line. A passing tug discharged some diesel oil into the canal, which I didn't see until it was too late. The line was absolutely destroyed and my efforts to clean it failed.

The fly line is our most important piece of equipment. Inexpensive reels are just fine and even a cheap rod will work in the hands of a good caster, but you've got to have a good line. Don't scrimp on that. Also, the warm-water enthusiast, like those who fish cold-water lakes, will require a much larger inventory of sinking lines than will the stream fisher.

REELS

The reel is relatively unimportant to the warm-water angler. I am aware that some leading authorities advocate putting bass on the reel. They say you can pick up the loose line fast enough with a multiplier reel, but I haven't been able to accomplish that feat. I lose the fish every time I try. They are either fishing in cleaner habitat than I am or they can crank awfully fast! (Anglers who mount the reel for left-hand cranking do have an advantage, however. I have never done any spin fishing and still mount my reel on the right; I have to switch hands to crank line and, admittedly, that takes a little time.) Bass are invariably hooked close to cover and you've got to horse them into the open quickly. There are probably ten or fifteen feet of loose line on the ground or deck when you hook the fish, which is joined by an additional ten feet when you yank him out of the cover. Remember that you cannot let these fellows run out the line like a river trout or a bonefish—you must hold them tightly or they will wrap around the nearest stick-up or become hopelessly ensnarled in weeds and moss. To stand there in the presence of all those hazards, hanging on to that hot fish while trying to pick up twenty-five or thirty feet of line, even with a 3:1 multiplier, just doesn't make any sense to me; it invariably results in disaster. Believe me, I've been there too many times. The astute reader knows the master angler to whom I refer, and I want to emphasize that I cut my warm-water teeth on his teachings; my admiration and respect is untarnished by my inability to play bass on the reel as he advocates. Perhaps someday he can personally show me how it's done—meanwhile I shall continue to play them by hand.

My advice, then, is to forget about the reel. If you don't stand on the line and learn to use the fingers of your line hand as a drag, you can bring the bass to net much more quickly and efficiently. There is, to be sure, a certain pleasurable feeling in playing a good fish on the reel, but I am afraid that it's a luxury we can't afford in most southern habitat. The same is true, incidentally, of a big bream on light tackle.

I prefer a lightweight reel and for years used the inexpensive Martin MG3, which was the lightest reel I could find (they don't make it anymore but still offer the lightest reels around). Most of my rods now carry Hardy reels, which are also light, for no other reason than the fact that it seemed inappropriate to put a thirty-dollar reel on a four-hundred-dollar rod! My Hardy Marquis, however, has the loudest click I have ever heard. It's actually embarrassing when I strip line on a crowded lake—all heads turn in my direction!

Always buy enough extra spools with a new reel to accommodate the wide variety of lines you will need in warm water. To be completely equipped for big-lake bass fishing you will need five extra spools: one each for intermediate, slow, and fast-sinking lines and one each for long and short sink tips in addition to the floating line on the reel itself. If you are really an extremist, you may even "need" two more spools for a floating bass bug taper and a saltwater taper for the really big flies! And, of course, where great distance is required, one of those new bonefish lines may be necessary. There may even be times when a monocore "slime" line is called for as well. Seriously, it is advisable to buy enough spools when you purchase the reel because manufacturers often discontinue models. The spools you need may not be obtainable later.

LEADERS

I am not going to teach the reader how to tie knots. Instead, I'll briefly share a few of my experiences with terminal tackle. I have tried every single fad that came along to attach the butt to the fly line. I started with those horrible barbed devices, followed by a little plastic "football" with a hole in each end. I graduated to the nail knot and learned to wrap and coat it with Pliobond so it would run through the guides. Later I began threading the leader into the line with epoxy. I improved upon that with a knot where the leader exits the line, and finally found the "ultimate" answer by threading the line into a hollow, braided butt section with a loop on the end. I don't waste time with any of this nonsense anymore—I simply use the same bare nail knot that I used twenty years ago! In the final analysis, you won't beat a plain old nail knot.

Many of my warm-water cohorts use level leaders and thereby save a small fortune. I believe, however, that the taper is helpful even with the big bugs; of course, it is critical with smaller bream flies. The only time I use a short, level piece of monofilament is with the big, sinking bass flies and plastic lures. As Dave Whitlock often says, knots gather moss and debris in warm-water habitats and a knotless leader is preferable. At two dollars a pop, however, I find that frugality requires me to attach at least a couple of new tippets before changing leaders. I fought the barrel knot for years, but Chuck Tryon finally talked me into the surgeon's knot about ten years ago. The latter wastes a lot more leader, but it's the only way to attach a tippet to a "fat" butt section.

I find that the really big bass flies unroll best with a very hard leader material. I usually keep a supply of Climax six-foot bass leaders, but one day I ran out and was forced to build a leader from the Mason Hard monofilament that I use for weedguard material. It made a super leader—the bug laid out perfectly straight every cast and it was nearly impossible to pile the leader. There are a couple of drawbacks, though. The Mason Hard isn't very strong in relation to diameter (OX is only six-pound-test) and it takes a memory on the reel spool. Maxima, a semi-hard material, is a good choice for building your own leaders. The formulae are the same as for trout leaders.

There is no doubt that a loop is best on a large bass fly with a heavy tippet. The Duncan slip loop is difficult to reopen once it's pulled down tight by a fish or snag and tying it wastes a lot of tippet. I prefer the fixed loop that the bass men use. On smaller tippets I tie the quick, easy old jam (clinch) knot. I don't have any problems with it as long as I wet the leader material first. A dry leader will break when you pull down a jam knot.

7

THE BREAM-FISHER'S
FLY BOX

Several years ago, my good friend and master angler, Brooks Bouldin of Houston, had just finished demonstrating some complicated hair work to a group of bass fishermen in East Texas when someone remarked that such fancy work was "more for the fisherman than for the fish." Brooks responded that the same could be said of any kind of lure and went on to explain that fly tying is, and should be, fifty percent for the fisherman; that form and function should compliment each other in any field of human endeavor. Architects and designing engineers know that appearance is an important aspect of even the humblest structure, tool, or utensil as long as it doesn't detract from the utilitarian purposes of the object.

Gifted tiers sometimes get carried away with form at the expense of function. Those artfully tied, hard-bodied, realistic nymphs have not proved effective and have fallen into disrepute. Conversely, few of us are content simply to dub a little muskrat fur on a hook, however satisfied the fish may be with such a basic offering. The key is to tie the fly as aesthetically as possible without sacrificing performance.

We are seeing some beautifully tied bass flies these days, but they are sometimes overdressed and don't fish well. Skilled tiers, in their quest for aesthetic excellence, should avoid unnecessary frills that may impair performance. If the law of gravity is defied in hair-bug design, for example, the result is a beautiful fly that rides belly-up when saturated. The center of gravity changes when the fly is thoroughly wet.

Dahlbergs perform best when tied on the sparse side; too much dressing will inhibit diving. Practical tiers like Brian Camp of Fort Worth and Bill Lambing of Lufkin, Texas, are striving to develop patterns for the challenges we face in deep-water bass fishing. They have tempered their creativity with an appropriate ration of pragmatism and we should resist temptations to "improve" their patterns by adding plastic eyes, skirts, hackles, and legs, which serve only to impress our fellow anglers and probably detract from the effectiveness of the lure.

Fly tying can also be an art form with no pretense of practicality. We all enjoy viewing and admiring artistic flies; many of the best occupy places of honor on my tying-room walls. I do feel, as Poul Jorgensen has pointed out, that such flies should not be represented as functional fishing lures. These distinctions are quite clear in cold-water tying but have become increasingly fuzzy in the warm-water field in recent years because many expert trout tiers enjoy creating bass flies but have little actual warm-water fishing experience. Since one of the purposes of this book is to get these fellows out on the lake or pond, not only will they love the fishing but their flies will reflect the knowledge they gain. As we have seen in preceding chapters, warm-water habitat is infinitely richer in life forms than most high-elevation trout waters. Many of these organisms have never been duplicated at the vise and the opportunities presented to the creative tier are virtually limitless. This is a very fresh, dynamic field, especially in regard to sinking bass flies, and much of what I say here could well be ancient history in a few years.

We are also eclectic in our endeavors, drawing ideas from both cold- and saltwater tiers. Jimmy Nix utilizes the bent back concept in his frog designs; Brooks Bouldin has adapted the Zonker to warm water with great success; Bob Clouser's minnow is becoming legendary on the salt flats as well as southern lakes; and we are even drawing on the work of such classical tiers as Harry Darbee, Polly Rosborough, and Charlie Brooks. It may surprise the reader that the outstanding cold-water scholarship of Gary Borger is finding extensive application in our fishery. Of course, the contributions of our own Dave Whitlock are so monumental as to require several volumes of this size. I am not going to subject the reader to a reiteration of material that's readily available elsewhere, but rather restrict the following discussion to the contents of my own fly box and present several patterns that I have developed through the years. The reader is referred to the bibliography for the titles containing the Whitlock and Borger patterns discussed in the preceding text. The tying sequences below are not intended for beginning tiers and assume basic skills.

FATHEAD DIVER

Larry Dahlberg's diving minnow is the most important development in warm-water tying since Joe Messinger, Sr., tied his first frog. Larry has given us an original, basic design that's adaptable and can imitate all sorts of surface organisms from a two-inch minnow to a foot-long water snake. Most of our so-called "new" patterns are simply modifications of existing ones, but occasionally genuine originality flowers in a gifted tier. Larry Dahlberg is destined to join that pantheon of revered fly fishers who have made lasting, monumental contributions to our sport.

This little fly, featured in *American Angler* magazine (July/August, 1991), was inspired by the fathead minnow. Commonly stocked in southern farm ponds, these little fellows school in great numbers in shoreside vegetation, sometimes in mere inches of water. Small bass patrol these weedlines, ready to inhale any hapless minnow that strays too far from the protective cover. I needed a weedless streamer that I could cast into the weeds and dart it out into deeper water. I tried tying a weedguard on the Marabou Muddler, but it didn't adapt well and the fly lacked buoyancy—it got too far down in the weeds and hung up. A very small Dahlberg was the obvious choice.

I had to compromise the effectiveness of the weedguard, however, by opening the loop larger than normal. I tied the weedguard in normal proportion initially, but I couldn't stick the fish. After dozens of missed strikes, I realized that the short span of hard mono was preventing hook point contact; it had become a fish guard. Only then did I remember a discussion of this very subject in Tom Nixon's classic *Fly Tying and Fly Fishing for Bass and Panfish*. I had been tying the guard one-third down the bend as we would on a larger sproat hook and keeping the mono fairly close to the hook point. Once I began tying the fly with a larger loop I started catching fish. I do have to adjust the guard regularly to keep it in line with the hook, and it doesn't do as good a job as on the larger flies, but it helps. I tie a weedguard on all my flies, but on those rare occasions that I find myself in clean water I clip it off. A weedguard detracts from the performance of any fly and should only be used when necessary.

FATHEAD DIVER

Hook: Mustad 3366, size 10
Threads: 6/0 black, 6/0 red
Weedguard: Mason #8 (.012)

Post:	Squirrel tail hair
Tail:	Brown over red marabou
Skirt:	Natural deer body hair tips
Collar:	Natural deer body hair
Body:	Natural deer body hair
Head:	6/0 black or brown tying thread

FATHEAD SHAD

Hook:	Mustad 3366, size 8
Thread:	6/0 yellow or cream
Weedguard:	Mason #8 (.012)
Post:	Yellow kiptail
Tail:	Cream marabou and pearl flashabou
Skirt:	Pale yellow or cream deer hair tips
Collar:	Pale yellow or cream deer body hair
Body:	Pale yellow or cream deer body hair
Head:	6/0 yellow or cream tying thread

FATHEAD FROG

Hook:	Mustad 3366, size 8
Thread:	6/0 yellow
Weedguard:	Mason #8 (.012)
Post:	Chartreuse kiptail
Tail:	Cree or grizzly hackle tips, splayed
Skirt:	Chartreuse deer hair tips
Collar:	Chartreuse deer body hair
Body:	Cream or pale yellow deer body hair
Head:	6/0 yellow thread

TYING SEQUENCES—FATHEAD DIVER

STEP 1   Flatten barb and sharpen the hook.

STEP 2   Using 6/0, tie in weedguard material at a point opposite the barb and extend back only a short way. Don't continue down the bend as we do on a larger hook; it will make the guard too stiff. Wrap a short thread base to the hook point—no farther. Cement.

While you're waiting for the cement on the weedguard windings to dry, keep in mind that there are three possible pitfalls on this little fly:

(1) not allowing a large enough loop on the weedguard; (2) failing to get the collar even and symmetrical, which causes the fly to float lopsided; and (3) getting too far forward with the tail windings and running out of hook shank to finish the body. Remember those three things as we continue.

STEP 3   Directly in front of the weedguard, on the short thread base, tie in a small clump of kiptail, or other stiff hair, as a post to prevent the marabou from wrapping around the hook. (I do this with all marabou patterns now—got the idea from Jimmy Nix.) Don't extend forward past the hook point.

STEP 4   Strip an appropriate amount of marabou from a plume, or other tailing materials, and tie in directly on top of the above windings, at a length about one and a half times the shank length. You'll learn the correct amount—don't get the windings too "fat." Cement these windings. At this point, you can switch to 3/0 thread if you must, but I continue with the 6/0. Many warm-water anglers are so used to tying huge bugs with "A" monocord that they have a hard time spinning hair with 6/0. Trout tiers will have an easier time with the finer thread. If you can stay with the 6/0, it will prevent bulky buildup.

STEP 5   Select a small amount of deer body hair for the skirt. Comb out the fuzzy underhair and even the tips in the stacker. Tie this directly on top of the tail windings. The length should be about half the tail. You can leave the butts to form part of the collar or trim them off—leaving them helps hide the windings on the finished fly. Take a couple of half-hitches and cement. There should be no windings forward of the hook point. If there are, strip it off and start again.

STEP 6   Select another clump for the collar. Comb, trim tips and butts. Cut it shorter than the skirt—it will be a lot easier to trim later. Now, you can stack this on top of the shank or you can spin it. If you spin, the hair will hit the hook point and you'll have to clear it with the dubbing needle. In any case, it must be evenly distributed and symmetrical. Don't pack too tightly; just snug it up. Different colors can be used for the collar and body. Some tiers find it easier to trim, but the one-color design   allows me to even up the collar with the razor blade. I have more latitude in trimming. With separate colors, I'm stuck with what I have. Also, I think one color looks more natural.

STEP 7   Spin and pack several more clumps, leaving only enough room to attach the weedguard. Use the less desirable parts of the hide—

no point in wasting that choice, long stuff. Don't pack it real tight as we do with the larger bugs. The hair gets so dense that it's hard to trim—you can't get rid of the "flat spots."

STEP 8   Remove from vise and trim in the Dahlberg style. Use a new, sharp blade and work carefully. Unlike the larger bugs, a little slip here and you've ruined the fly!

STEP 9   Return to vise and tie off the weedguard with 6/0. You can't bring the mono through the eye and fold it over as we do on larger hooks—the eye is too small. Instead, run the mono through the eye and pull it snug to the hook point; take four or five loose turns and cut the mono about 6 mm above the eye (you'll learn the correct amount). Then pull the mono down until it just clears the eye and take a couple of tighter turns to secure it. Make sure it's straight and in line on the bottom side. Whip finish and cement. Remove from vise and coat collar with cement.

FENCE RIDERS

The reader will recall the discussion of the "bass or bream dilemma" in Chapter 6. As a farm-pond angler, I am frequently fishing waters that have a mixture of bream and small (under three pounds in Texas) largemouth bass. Although bass will occasionally take a dry fly or other diminutive offering, the old, "big fly, big fish" rule does seem to apply to this species. Common twelve- to fifteen-inch pond bass will take a standard hair bug or other large fly readily, but the heavy tackle required to cast them is overkill on such waters. The angler completely closes the door on the bluegill. On the other hand, small nymphs and dries fished on two- and three-weight gear will interest few bass. My so-

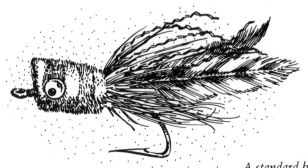

A standard bass hair bug

lution to this dilemma is to scale down standard bass flies to a size 6 sproat hook. Six seems to be an awkward number in fly fishing. A six-weight is sort of "funky" on a trout stream; it's too light for bass and too heavy for bluegill. Likewise, size 6 hooks are too small for bass fishing and too large for most bluegills. Therein lies the efficacy of the intermediate size. The size 6 bug may not be a full meal for the bass, but it's substantial enough to bring him up. Small bream will inspect such a fly, and the big boys, the ones we are primarily interested in, will have no problem taking it. These patterns will cast on a five-weight line easily, and they enable me to "ride the fence" between bass and bream. Another old cliché applies here as well—I can "have my cake and eat it too."

FENCE RIDER BUG (all colors optional)

Hook:	Mustad 3366, size 6
Thread:	6/0 black and 3/0 monocord black
Weedguard:	Mason #8 (.012)
Post:	Fox squirrel tail hair
Tail:	Brown marabou and two cree or grizzly hackle tips, splayed
Skirt:	Olive deer body hair tips
Body:	Alternating bands of natural and olive deer body hair
Eyes:	3mm yellow/black hollow doll eyes

FENCE RIDER DIVER (all colors optional)

Hook:	same as above
Threads:	" " "
Weedguard:	" " "
Post:	" " "
Tail:	" " "
Skirt:	" " "
Collar:	Olive deer body hair
Body:	Natural deer body hair
Eyes:	4 mm (smaller if you can find them) solid plastic eyes

TYING SEQUENCES—FENCE RIDER BUG

STEP 1   Crimp barb and sharpen hook.

STEP 2   Using 6/0, attach weedguard at a point opposite the hook point. Extend windings only a short distance down the bend to prevent the weedguard from being *too* efficient. Wrap a short thread base immediately forward of the weedguard tie-in point. Cement these windings and let it dry.

STEP 3   Select a small clump of squirrel tail for the post, even the tips, and attach directly on top of the thread base. Use minimal number of turns. This should be about the same length as the hook shank.

STEP 4   Tie a generous clump of marabou fibers directly on top of the post windings. Make them about one-and-a-half times the shank length. Take minimal turns.

STEP 5   Select two matching hackle tips from the same neck. Even the tips and clip the butts to a length twice the hook shank. Do not trim or strip barbules. Attach each feather separately, on either side of the existing windings, to form a splayed tail. Whip finish and cement.

STEP 6   Attach 3/0 monocord on cemented windings. Select a sparse clump of deer hair for the skirt, even the tips, and stack directly on top of the same windings at a length slightly shorter than the marabou. Take a couple of loose turns to lay the skirt down somewhat.

STEP 7   Advance thread to the bare shank ahead of the above windings. Take a couple of half-hitches on the bare shank to prevent heavy tail materials from "rolling" when you spin the hair. Spin several clumps of deer hair to the eye, leaving only enough room to attach the weedguard later.

STEP 8   Remove from vise and trim the bottom flat as you would with a larger bug. Using a small piece of plastic bag as a hackle guard, attach the weedguard in the same manner as in Step 9 of the Fathead Diver instructions. Thoroughly coat the face of the bug with head cement until all the hair is lying nice and flat. Let this dry overnight.

STEP 9   The face should be about one centimeter wide. Clip both bottom reference lines as you would with any hair bug, but don't taper—go straight back. Then, following the reference lines, trim straight down the sides with the razor blade parallel to the hook. In other words, the body will now be square on three sides.

STEP 10   Make a small indentation with a wood burner or scissors at each front-bottom corner of the partially trimmed bug just large enough to receive 4 mm doll eyes. Attach eyes with Goop or five-minute epoxy.

When the eyes have dried, trim the top of the bug with the razor blade. Start just above the eyes and taper this cut toward the rear. Be careful not to cut tail windings or skirt.

STEP 11   Using curved scissors, round off all sharp corners on the back, face, and sides of the bug.

The fly is now ready to fish. I have found the above methods, especially trimming the back after the eyes have been attached, to be a lot easier on very small hair bugs. Also, trimming goes a lot better if the untrimmed face is cemented first. Tying the Fence Rider Diver is essentially the same as the Fathead Diver on a larger hook.

DIXIE McDOUGALS

Warm-water fly tying is an eclectic art and we lean heavily on our trout-fishing progenitors. Where would we bream fishers be without our muddlers and hoppers? It seems quite unlikely that one of our most effective farm-pond patterns originated on the banks of the fabled Beaverkill, but Harry Darbee's Rat-Faced McDougal is indispensable in the bream angler's box. Originally named Beaverkill Bastards (Darbee recognized that these flies were actually a cross between a bass fly and a standard dry), I have further bastardized the pattern into Dixie Mc-Dougals. They have proved very effective in representing several Hymenoptera that are common around warm-water ponds. I can only hope that Harry's not spinning in his grave.

A McDougal-type fly

WASP McDOUGAL

Hook: Mustad 94840, size 8 (Use lighter wire for high flotation)
Thread: 6/0 black
Tail: Orange bucktail, tied full to suggest the abdominal configuration of the wasp
Body: Reddish-brown deer body hair
Wing: Black hackle tips, tied long—perhaps 2 cm
Hackle: Grizzly, cree, or domestic variant, dyed orange
Head: 6/0 black thread

BUMBLE McDOUGAL

Hook: Mustad 9671, size 8 (This insect will likely be trapped in the surface film and the heavier wire will give a saturated appearance.)
Thread: Same as above
Tail: The brownish center of a dyed yellow buck tail. Not as full as the wasp.
Body: Alternating bands of black and yellow deer hair, trimmed fatter and bulkier than the wasp. Be sure to leave enough gape to permit hook point contact.
Wing: Cree or grizzly hackle tips, shorter and wider than the wasp
Hackle: Grizzly, cree, or domestic variant, dyed yellow, or one yellow and one black hackle
Head: 6/0 black

MUD DAUBER McDOUGAL

Hook: Mustad 94840 or 9671, size 8
Thread: Same as above
Tail: Black bucktail, tied full to suggest the wasp-like configuration
Body: Deer body hair, dyed blue
Wing: Cree or grizzly hackle tips
Hackle: Black, or one black and one blue
Head: 6/0 black

These flies should be fished with no retrieve, but a little "jiggling" movement will simulate a struggling insect. Use the wasp pattern directly under pondside nests (keep your distance!), especially in early summer. The bee is most productive during the gorgeous displays of flowering water plants that grace southern waters each spring, but they are common around the pond all year, even on sunny winter days. The metallic-blue mud-dauber wasp frequents muddy pond edges all summer and since sunfish are quite used to seeing them the imitation is a good searching pattern. As with any deer-hair fly, color variations are limitless. I tie them in olive, chartreuse, basic black, and everybody's warm-water favorite, red and white.

There is no way I can improve on Dick Talleur's tying instructions for the McDougal-type fly. The reader is referred to his *Versatile Fly Tyer* for the do's and don'ts of these patterns. Dick deals only with Darbee's original pattern, of course, but the only difference is color.

MINI-BUGS

I also tie miniature bugs on Mustad 3366, size 8. Materials and procedures are identical to the Fence Rider. Use the same weedguard material as on the Fathead Diver and keep the same open loop that I recommend on all these small deer-hair flies. Use 3 mm doll eyes, which are available in most craft stores. Just drop the Fence Rider proportions one size.

These little bugs are useful in imitating various terrestrials, especially mid-sized beetles and the true bugs (Hemiptera). Even certain hoppers and crickets are well represented by mini-bugs. We encounter a wide variety of organisms in warm water, and it is not uncommon to find some "off the wall" species present on the pond in considerable numbers. The warm-water angler needs a variety of impressionistic flies in his box in order to address these situations. I tie mini-bugs in black, natural, olive, brown, and chartreuse.

Grasshopper

A Water Pup-type fly

GRINNEL FLY

I wrote an article a few years ago on fly fishing for bowfin, which are colloquially called "grinnel" in Texas (*American Angler*, Fall 1990). The variation of the Whitlock Hare Water Pup that I presented in the article is an excellent imitation of a juvenile water snake and has proved to be a very effective bass fly in both its wet and dry form. It differs from Dave's original pattern only in the smaller head and longer, thinner rabbit-strip tail. It is, in essence, a sparsely tied Water Pup. Natrix water snakes are eight to ten inches long at birth. While this fly is only half that length, it still does a credible job of simulating the organism and is a lot easier to cast than a life-size snake. You can tie this fly on a larger hook, but the rabbit strip gets so heavy when saturated that you'll have to use an eight- or nine-weight to cast it. This pattern handles comfortably on a six-weight.

I prefer natural rabbit strips with the white hide. Dying turns the hide dark, usually quite black, which is completely unnatural—a snake's venter is always light in coloration. Also, colors can be added to the underside of the strip with a Pantone marker to better represent certain species that may have green or orange venters. As with any fly, colors are completely optional and depend on the species of water snakes present in any given lake. In my own experience, natural brown rabbit and natural deer hair have been an unbeatable combination everywhere I have fished.

DRESSING FOR GRINNEL FLY (colors optional)

Hook: Mustad 3366, size 2
Thread: 3/0 monocord, black
Weedguard: .019 hard monofilament
Tail: Thin, natural brown rabbit strip, about 4″ long
Collar: Natural deer body hair tips
Body: Natural deer body hair
Eyes: 4 mm doll eyes
Head: 3/0 black monocord

TYING SEQUENCES—GRINNEL FLY

STEP 1   Crimp the barb and sharpen hook.

STEP 2   Tie in weedguard at about the middle of the shank, or even a little forward of the middle. You want a small head, so keep it well forward. Extend windings back about one-third down the bend and return, making a small thread base just ahead of the weedguard butt. Cement and let it dry.

STEP 3   Cut the rabbit strip very thin with a razor blade, following the natural direction of the hair. The thinner you can cut it the better the fly will cast. About 3 mm is good. Pre-cut strips are generally too wide and must be cut in half.

STEP 4   Tie in the strip on the thread base, directly on top of the hook. Make sure the hair is lying backward in the right direction. Cement.

STEP 5   Select a sparse clump of deer hair and even the tips. Take two *loose* turns and spin the collar completely around the windings. It's difficult to spin hair on a thread base and it takes a little practice. The secret is in using light tension.

The collar can also be stacked directly on top of the windings; the fly doesn't look as good, but fishes the same. The tips should not extend past the bend of the hook. Take several loose turns to lay the collar down.

STEP 6   Spin and pack several clumps of hair to the eye, leaving only enough room to tie off the weedguard. Remove from vise.

STEP 7   Using scissors, rough-cut body to a slender, torpedo shape. Finish with sharp razor blade.

STEP 8   Return to vise. Tie off weedguard, whip finish, and cement.

STEP 9   Make an indentation with a wood burner or scissors to accept 4 mm doll eyes. Place the eyes far forward, near the eye of the hook and affix them with Goop or epoxy. Either hollow or solid eyes can be used, depending upon the amount of buoyancy desired.

This is the most effective bass pattern in my box. Neutral buoyancy can easily be achieved by trimming and by the type of eyes selected. The fly should be slightly buoyant so it will ride low in the surface film when fished topwater and it should be tied with neutral buoyancy when fished near the bottom on a sinking line. I tie them in various colors but the above pattern is by far the most productive in my waters. This fly looks so realistic slithering through the weeds, you'll have to resist the urge to eat it yourself!

BROOKS BOULDIN'S CRAPPIE FLY

Hook:	Mustad 3906B, size 4
Thread:	3/0 monocord, black
Eyes:	1/50 oz. lead eyes, painted black
Body:	Pearlescent sparkle braid
Tail:	White calf tail

STEP 1   Tie on lead eyes, approximately 1/8 inch back from eye.

STEP 2   Tie in tail, immediately behind eyes. Length should extend just past the bend, curving downward a bit.

STEP 3   Tie in sparkle braid on top of tail windings. With sparkle braid lying parallel to hook shank, overwrap these materials to a point opposite the barb. The single strand of sparkle braid and the calf hair will help form the body. Advance the thread back to the eye of the hook.

STEP 4   Wind the sparkle braid forward in close wraps, crisscrossing the lead eyes with figure 8, to a point forward of the eyes.

STEP 5   Tie off the sparkle braid, form a neat head, whip finish and cement.

BILL LAMBING'S HAIRY MOUSE SLIDER

Hook:	Mustad 37189, heavy wire stinger, size 10
Thread:	Black monocord, size "A"

Weedguard: Stiff monofilament (optional). Bill ties this fly without a weedguard

Tail: 8–9 inch chamois strip, cut very thin—perhaps 2 mm

Skirt: Natural deer hair, tips left on. Long hair is required 2 to 2½ inches

Body: Natural deer hair, spun and clipped

Head: Tying thread

STEP 1   Attach weedguard if desired.

STEP 2   Tie in chamois strip at a point opposite the barb.

STEP 3   Select a generous clump of very long natural deer hair. Even the tips and *stack* this directly on top of the tail windings. The tips should extend way back—twice the shank length or more. Do not flair more than necessary. Advance the thread forward of the short butts and wind a short thread base to stack the next clump. Do not trim the butts.

STEP 4   Select another similar clump, even the tips, and stack on the short thread base directly in front of the first clump. This clump should be slightly shorter than the first one. Advance thread—do not trim the short butts. Gently pack and add a drop of cement.

STEP 5   Spin successive clumps of deer hair to the eye, leaving enough room for the head and/or weedguard tie-off. Cement each clump. Trim with scissors—no razor blade—for an intentional rough look.

STEP 6   Trim the bottom to a rounded, oval shape, leaving just enough gape for the hook to function. This is the reason for the wide gape hook.

STEP 7   Clip the sides and top of the fly at a thirty-degree angle, from the eye upward. The result will be a ragged-looking, ugly fly. Bill says it looks like it came from the trash can at a beginner's tying clinic. The fly is also out of proportion, appearing much too large for the size 10 stinger hook. This is intentionally done to maximize the natural texture and reduce rejection. I made fun of the fly when Bill first tied it, but changed my tune after his first eight-pounder!

Bill came to my house on a miserably cold, windy November day to help me with the above tying sequences. My tying bench overlooks a bass pond and we joked about the futility of going fishing under such adverse conditions. After he tied a couple of Hairy Mouse Sliders, we walked down to the pond, bundled up in coats and hats, so Bill could demonstrate his retrieve techniques. On the second cast a twelve-inch bass clobbered the fly. I was incredulous; topwater action in this cold water? Impossible! Soon he had another on the line. We got in the boat and Bill connected with seven fish in fifteen minutes. Use a Duncan or fixed loop to attach this fly.

This slider should be retrieved rather fast on a floating line. It also fishes well on a sinking line, riding high off the bottom. As pointed out elsewhere, texture is the key variable in deep-water bass fishing and the ragged, soft, bushy nature of this fly apparently feels lifelike in the fish's mouth. It is very buoyant and skates across the surface, but dives on a sink tip. Bill doesn't let it sit, like a bug, but begins the retrieve as soon as the fly hits the water. He knows I don't like attractors; I prefer to imitate actual food forms. When I asked what this represents, he responded, with a nearly straight face, that it is a field mouse that has been accidentally dropped by a female red-tail hawk on her way to the nest. I guess that will work.

WASP LARVA

Without question, the deadliest, most universally effective bait for bluegills are fresh larvae from the nest of red wasps. In any warm-water habitat, sunfishes go berserk over any sort of grub-like morsel, wasp larvae in particular. My rural neighbors have devised all sorts of ingenious ways to distract the wasps long enough to rob the nest (blow torches, boiling water, CO_2 fire extinguishers, or, for the less creative, batting the nest down with a long stick and running like hell) without spoiling the bait with insecticides. This is dangerous business; it's much safer to tie a fly to represent the natural.

Since the larva is just a little white blob of protoplasm, this is the easiest of all flies to tie. Simply form a dubbing loop, wax it a little, and put a small amount of cream-colored lamb's wool, or any light cream dubbing material, in the loop. Twist it and wind it onto a size 14 dry fly hook so it will sink slowly. Clip off any stray fibers of wool. That's it! Though the fly doesn't look like much, it will take more bream than anything else in your box. Naturally, I would never consider such a thing, but I have "this friend," you see, who mashes real larvae into a liquid and soaks these flies in that for a few days. The resulting, badly compromised, "fly" is as close to a sure thing as one can ever get in fly fishing.

MARABOU MUDDLERS

All fly fishers have a special fly that they know will do the job when all else fails. Mine is the Marabou Muddler. This is the design I use for all my streamers, varying coloration accordingly. I have seen this fly tied with a huge deer-hair body and a lot of fluffy dressing. This is not the version I use; it floats on top of the water like a bug! My idea of a Marabou Muddler is that presented by Utah tier Terry Hellekson in his *Popular Fly Patterns*. When properly tied, these flies neither sink nor float; they are neutrally buoyant. Depth, if desired, is achieved with a sinking line, leader, or split shot; I don't tie lead into the fly, which spoils its action. With a number of colors in sizes 6 to 10, I can effectively represent all of the fifty-plus species of baitfish that occur in my part of the Lone Star state. Rather than plagiarize Terry's book, I simply refer the reader to that source.

OTHER STANDARDS

Woolly Worms are crucial in the bream-fisher's box, especially later in the season when arboreal Lepidoptera are most abundant. Most of these larvae are either smooth or bristled; only a few are actually hackled. Nonetheless, I tie a sparse hackle on all my Woolly Worms and clip or trim them accordingly while fishing. Keep it sparse, though, by either stripping the barbules from one side of the hackle feather or palmering widely. The standard chenille body is hard to beat and it is adaptable to any color combination. The larvae vary widely in size during developmental stages, but they don't drop from the tree until mature (see Chapter Five). We are primarily concerned with worms that are sizes 6 and 8. Mustad 9672 is the hook of choice here. They should not be weighted when tied on heavy wire—most takes occur as the worm slowly sinks and tumbles toward the bottom.

Nymphs are equally important in the warm-water arsenal, especially Odonata imitations in sizes 6 to 10. Fair Damsel and Dragon are good basic patterns and are also found in *Popular Fly Patterns*. Jeff Hines, of Dallas, recently introduced me to Polly Rosborough's Casual Dress. Jeff ties the fly with a soft hackle, and it is proving very effective for me. Craig Mathews' Crane Fly Larvae is also a staple in my box and has numerous warm-water applications. I confess that my expertise in tying nymphs is marginal at best. My specialty is deer-hair work, and I trade my divers, bugs, and McDougals to other tiers for nymphs. Since

A soft-hackle nymph

every tier normally has an area of specialization, this sort of swapping arrangement works very well for all parties.

I also carry a variety of standard dries, especially Adams, California Mosquito, and Joe's Hopper in sizes 12 and 14, Black Ant in size 16, Dave's Hopper in 6 and 8, and standard Rat-Faced McDougals in size 8. Other impressionistic cold-water flies are useful from time to time. The bream fisher is well-advised to carry a few Renegades, Bivisibles, Humpies, and Irresistibles in a variety of sizes and colors. There are also a few sponge spiders and mini-jigs hidden in my box, but no Sneaky Petes or Dixie Devils!

WARM-WATER WOOLLY WORMS

The southern angler will encounter many brightly marked species of arboreal Lepidoptera. The opportunities for creative fly tying are almost endless for the warm-water angler, and the following patterns represent a few common organisms.

FALL WEBWORM

Hook:	9672, size 12
Thread:	6/0 white
Tail:	None
Body:	Cream lamb's wool
Overbody:	Olive chenille
Hackle:	Cream
Head:	6/0 white

WALNUT CATERPILLAR

Hook:	Mustad 79580, size 6, bent slightly
Thread:	6/0 black
Tail:	Goose biot segment, black
Body:	Black chenille
Overbody:	Yellow chenille

A Caterpillar and Catalpa Worm-type fly

Underbody: Yellow chenille
Hackle: Black—stripped on one side and clipped closely on
              finished fly
Head: One turn red chenille. Finish with tying thread.

GREEN OAKWORM

Hook: Tiemco 200R, size 10
Thread: 6/0 black
Tail: Goose biot segments, olive
Body: Olive lamb's wool
Rib: Olive Larva Lace
Head: One turn black chenille, finish with 6/0 black

CATALPA WORM

Hook: Mustad 79580, size 6, bent slightly
Thread: 6/0 black
Tail: Goose biot segments, black
Body: Cream or pale yellow lamb's wool
Overbody: Black chenille
Hackle: Black, stripped on one side and clipped closely
              on the finished fly
Head: 6/0 black

TYING WITH NEUTRAL BUOYANCY

As discussed in preceding chapters, neutrally buoyant flies are indispensable in still, warm water. I trim the head on my Marabou Muddlers, for example, so the buoyant deer hair just balances the weight of the hook. The result is a fly that not only alleviates the snag problems of a sinking fly, but also more effectively imitates baitfish that move in short darts, punctuated by motionless pauses. The Grinnel Fly is deadliest when presented on a sinking line, trimmed to neither sink nor float. A waterlogged terrestrial that slips below the surface film is taken more readily than a floating natural. Still-water trout fishers are also discovering the advantages of tying with neutral buoyancy. Colorado angler Mike Tucker has developed a series of liquid-bodied flies that will find many warm-water applications. He fills polyurethane tubing with vegetable oil and uses that as an underbody. Vegetable oil floats, of course, and balances the weight of the hook. My wife puts up with hair and feathers, but she might balk at Wesson oil all over the floor!

I have spent many hours watching large bluegills feed on naturals. It's not unusual for a nine-inch fish to circle a floating terrestrial for a full minute; he'll inspect it from every angle, and perhaps sipping it in and blowing it out a couple of times to make sure he likes it, before eating the insect. Unless there is a hatch in progress to trigger competitive, aggressive behavior, taking bluegills on a dry is difficult. Slow-sinking naturals, however, appear to be taken with gusto. After a frustrating weekend of watching such discerning behavior, experienced trout fisher and talented fly tier Jeff Hines, of Dallas, sat down at my vise and tied a fly that works incredibly well. His SS (Slow-Sinking) Damsel has been taking big bluegills and redears like a live garden worm! I've caught so many fish in front of my house on his pattern that they are starting to recognize it as an imitation.

SS DAMSEL

Hook:	Tiemco 200, size 10 or 12
Thread:	8/0 black
Tail:	Marabou fibers, olive
Underbody:	Polycelon foam or fly foam
Overbody:	Dubbed Antron, dark olive or olive-gray
Rib:	Pearl or Light Green Crystal Flash
Underwing:	Two strands of pearl or light green Crystal Flash on each side of thorax, trimmed to length of body
Hackle:	Hungarian partridge body feather, very sparse
Head:	Tying thread

STEP 1   Crimp barb and sharpen the hook. Wrap a thread base on the entire shank.

STEP 2   Strip a few fluffy fibers from a marabou plume for the tail and tie in slightly aft of barb. These should be fairly long, perhaps one-third the shank length.

STEP 3   Cut a strip of Polycelon foam sheeting approximately 3 mm wide. Tie in directly in front of tail windings and wrap around the shank to form abdomen and a fatter thorax. Tie off behind the eye, leaving enough room for hackle and head. Crisscross the foam with tying thread for durability but don't overdo it. If you bind it down too tightly it will lose its buoyant characteristic. Return thread to the tail windings.

STEP 4   Tie in a single strand of Crystal Flash for the rib. Then, using a dubbing loop, overwrap foam underbody with Antron dubbing for about two-thirds the shank length to form abdomen. Advance rib and tie off at this point. Continue dubbing to cover the rest of the foam underbody.

STEP 5   Tie in two strands of Crystal Flash, the length of the shank, each side of thorax. Select a Hungarian partridge body feather for the hackle and strip off all but five to six fibers on each side. Tie in directly in front of the thorax. The natural curve of the fibers should be toward the rear. Wind hackle. Form a small head with the tying thread, whip finish, and cement.

This combination of foam and wire comes close to achieving the near neutral buoyancy that we need. Jeff is still looking for material that is even more buoyant than the Polycelon and will welcome suggestions. Many patterns can be tied with the foam underbody. I have tied and successfully fished an SS Crane Fly Larva, an SS Wasp Larva (especially deadly on bluegills), and an SS Catalpa Worm.

Polly Rosborough's Casual Dress has proved to be an excellent impressionistic nymph in our fishery, and I think it will adapt well to the foam underbody. Dubbed muskrat patterns all have a special place in my heart. Back in the 1960s, when I was fishing the then pristine waters of southwest Montana, I didn't enjoy fly tying. It was a burdensome chore necessitated by lack of funds, and I always took the easiest way out. I found that I could simply dub a little muskrat on a hook (no hackle, no tail) and create a nymph that was as effective as anything in Dan Bailey's bins. I take more pride in my flies now, of course, but tying Casual Dress brings back many precious memories of hundreds of wild trout that fell for those ratty old muskrat flies. Jeff has given us a basic design concept, and I expect to eventually have a whole "fleet" of SS (slow-sink) flies. Meanwhile, Darlene has hidden the cooking oil and is praying that the Polycelon foam continues to work!

TYING WARM-WATER ANTS

Ant imitations are crucial in the trout fisher's box, and the cold-water literature is replete with patterns in both winged and non-winged forms. Although a store-bought foam body, tied on a hump-shank hook with a couple of turns of hackle at the waist, may be functional in warm water, I prefer a more sophisticated tie with natural materials. I can form the segmented body with dubbed fur in the Borger-style, but his parachute hackle is not in my tying repertoire. I use Mike Lawson's Fur Ant, an easily tied variation with hackle tip wings (*American Angler*, Fall 1990). The three basic colors that Mike uses on the Henry's Fork—black, mahogany-brown, and cinnamon-red—will cover all the species encountered on southern waters.

Juvenile sunfish present a problem when fishing small dry flies. Little bluegills are more surface-oriented than mature fish, and they grab the fly the instant it hits the water. It's very frustrating when a four-inch bluegill darts out of the weeds and snatches the dry away from that rising big shadow that you're breathlessly watching. This situation arises whenever I attempt to address the primary aspects of any insect emergence or terrestrial phenomenon. A partial solution is to use an oversize fly, perhaps several times larger than the natural. Mike's Fur Ant, in cinnamon-red, is an excellent imitation of the fire ant in size 20, but experience has taught me that such a fly will take few quality fish. The same ant tied on a size 12 will tend to discourage the little guys and give me a chance at that ten-inch slab. The guiding rule is to go as large as possible. The concept of "big fly-big fish" has greater validity in warm-water fisheries than on trout streams, but is not completely alien there either. I used to get past the little rainbows on California's Mokelumne River by presenting big Irresistibles to the few resident browns. I didn't catch many browns . . . but I did get past the rainbows!

HENRY'S FORK HOPPER

I am sure Mike Lawson never envisioned a warm-water application for this pattern, but it has proved important in our fishery on several occasions. In addition to the "retrieved hopper" application discussed in Chapter 3, I have since encountered both bass and bream that simply wouldn't take anything else! The following tying instructions appeared in *American Angler & Fly Tyer* magazine in the Fall 1990 issue, and Mike has kindly given me permission to reprint them here.

Hook:	TMC 5212 2X1, sizes 8 to 14
Thread:	Yellow 3/0 waxed monocord
Abdomen:	Cream or yellow elk hair tied in at the thorax. Wrap the thread back to the bend of the hook, and continue wrapping the thread back over the elk hair until the body extends one-quarter of the length of the hook

shank past the bend of the hook. Now pull the hair forward over these thread wraps, distributing the hair evenly around the "underbody" and spiral wrap the thread forward over the hair, forming the segments of the body. Tie off the thread at the thorax.

Underwing:	Yellow or olive elk hair.
Overwing:	Mottled hen-saddle feather or pheasant-rump feather coated with Dave's Flexament
Head and Thorax:	Natural light-gray elk hair pulled back from the eye of the hook to form a bullet-shaped head. The head should be one-quarter of the length of the body, and the hair forming the collar should extend two-thirds of the length of the body. Clip the collar hair on the bottom.

8

CONCLUSIONS AND PREDICTIONS

I have sought in the preceding pages to present southern warm-water fly fishing as a truly viable alternative for my northern brothers and sisters of the angle. That has been my intent, as stated in the introduction, and I pray that my pleas are accepted because, to be brutally frank, it probably will be the only fishing we will have in the coming century. It was convenient and fashionable to look down our noses at "panfish" when we enjoyed countless miles of pristine, unpolluted trout streams. Fly fishing has been inextricably linked with the salmonoids for 500 years and applying our efforts to a new and different fishery requires some soul-searching emotional and intellectual adjustments. I cut my fly-fishing teeth on trout streams and had a difficult time changing my attitude until I realized that sunfish are a lot harder to catch than I had assumed. I was truly astounded at the level of sophistication that they really demanded, and now I regret that I didn't look at this challenging fishery many years ago. As in a second marriage, one has to accept warm-water species for what they are; you gradually learn not to compare them continually with trout. Although these fishes compare quite favorably in many respects, this is an unfair approach. One will not truly enjoy fishing for them until he overcomes it. My respect and admiration for the sunfishes has grown with each day on the pond, and they now occupy a place in my heart alongside our beloved trouts. You will fall in love with them too, if you only give them a chance.

Unfortunately, it may only be a matter of time until the largemouth bass goes the way of the rainbow trout and succumbs to hatchery domestication. Given their penchant for minnows and crawfish, it has never been economically feasible to raise bass in hatcheries, but aquaculturists are finding ways around that. A few private hatcheries are now breeding bass that will eat pellets. They put fingerlings in a sterile tank and feed them only a specially formulated ration. Most refuse to eat the dry food and die, but the few survivors that thrive reproduce offspring with even less-discriminating tastes. The fattened bass then are shipped live to major cities where they fetch a very high price in Asian-American communities. Fortunately, so far this activity has been restricted to the fresh fish market. I do not anticipate that any of the bream species will ever be a factor on the fresh fish market. They are too small, too slow-growing, and too boney to ever be marketed as food fish. Hopefully, they will never interest fish farmers or public hatcheries.

I have recently had an opportunity to observe the behavior of some of the "new" hatchery-raised bass that were experimentally stocked in a small pond. They behaved just like hatchery rainbows. They were incredibly easy to catch; they stayed together in a school and were unable to adapt to the new environment. This behavior created trauma for the wild fish, which fled to the far end of the pond. The "new" bass refused to eat anything but pellets and were extremely vulnerable to a family of otters that resided nearby. They generally proved very unsatisfactory as game fish. Fortunately, the new bass exhibited learned behavior; their offspring will again be wild. In this case, the introduction of new bass was beneficial. The resident bass in that particular pond were not spawning. Fresh genetic material was needed, but attempts to correct the population with fingerlings failed—they were quickly eaten before they could adapt to the environment. So the adult hatchery bass were stocked for breeding purposes. However, I was surprised and deeply disappointed to find that it is possible to domesticate a bass. I guess nothing in nature is safe from modern technology.

The parents of those bass were wild and their offspring will be too, but genetic manipulation appears to be right around the corner. Scientists have now learned how to develop strains of gullible, easily caught bass. Some fish are naturally aggressive feeders and will grab any offering with reckless abandon; other individuals are careful, picky eaters that rarely will take a lure of any sort. Since these traits are genetic, the offspring of wary bass are even harder to catch than are their parents.

In a carefully controlled, six-year experiment at the Texas Parks and Wildlife Department Heart of the Hills research station, researchers discovered that though ten percent of wild, uneducated bass are quite gullible, nearly a quarter of them will never take a lure regardless of how hungry they are. Both groups, dubbed "wary" and "naive" by the scientists, were then separated and bred selectively. By the third generation, nearly half of the wary fish refused a lure; the naive group became correspondingly easier to catch with each generation. Intelligence seems to be as hereditary among fishes as it obviously is among dogs, horses, and humans.

Two-thirds of the original wild fish in the study were of average intelligence; they were catchable but also educable. They would fall for the same lure once or twice and then demand a different offering presented with more finesse—typical and predictable behavior. This is, of course, the segment of the population that we should encourage, but there is already talk of intentionally breeding gullible fish for stocking in public lakes. Fisheries managers will most likely succumb to this irresistible temptation. They are committed to providing the most fish for the greatest number, despite the opposition of the Sierra Club and most, if not all, of the bass clubs in Texas. There is even speculation that hatcheries may one day offer "designer" bass for differing levels of angling skill. We had better enjoy our wild, native bass while we can because the day is surely coming when it will be as hard to find a wild bass as a wild trout.

The study did shed some light on my own fishing. Apparently, we are inadvertently breeding strains of picky bass in our ponds and lakes when we remove aggressive individuals—the very ones most likely to take a topwater bug. I can take you to a lovely little lake that supports a very healthy population of uncatchable bass. You can throw flies, spinnerbaits, and plugs at these fish all day without results. A plastic worm will take an occasional fish, but only live bait will really produce. The pond has been fished with lures for decades, and the owners, following conventional wisdom, have regularly removed a few fish to prevent overpopulation. I had assumed that these bass were simply "educated," like the trout in a catch-and-release spring creek, but it may be that removing the most easily caught fish has created a population of exceptionally bright bass. Except for widespread, misguided attempts to improve upon Mother Nature through hybridization, the wild genes of bluegills and other bream are still intact, however, and will likely remain so well into the future.

One would have to live in a vacuum to be optimistic about the future of wild fish; indeed, man's own existence is in some doubt. Journalist Linda Ellerbee commented some years ago that 1955 was "the last year we could look into the future and not be afraid of what we saw." Our trout waters have been shrinking at an alarming rate in recent decades, and those that remain are subject to such heavy usage that limited access restrictions on some waters appear inevitable. Quality fly fishing in the coming century will be restricted to a privileged minority, and realistic environmentalists, most notably the Nature Conservancy, are recognizing that the only way we can save part of the natural world is to buy it and put a fence around it. (If the ozone layer disappears, we may have to encapsulate it in a building as well.) Fragile cold-water resources are the most seriously threatened, and we should applaud each mile of trout stream that goes behind posted signs. Even if we cannot fish there, just knowing it still exists is worth a lot. I know how Americans loathe this kind of European snobbery, but the harsh reality is that the only future alternative to private trout water is no water at all! Wildlife management agencies are struggling valiantly to detour this trend but the developing plot of "the tragedy, Man" is inexorably dragging us, kicking and screaming, into the twenty-first century. The misanthropic Poe never dreamed in his wildest, drug-induced hallucination that the hero of the play, the "conqueror worm," would itself be threatened on a planet awash with toxins.

Stephen Bodio, my favorite reviewer of fly-fishing books, has commented in his popular column that, in taking this view, I am giving up on wilderness and "ensuring defeat by conceding it in advance." I hate to agree with the doomsday philosophy that pervades my Bible Belt area, but I think it's quite clear that political, economic, and even biological realities ensure the ultimate destruction of what little public wilderness remains. Our efforts may slow down the dam builders, loggers, and miners, but we are little more than a thorn in their side. We may give the spotted owl a little more time today and stop a dam project tomorrow, but history has proven that the political climate will surely change and that economic considerations will always prevail in the end. Even as I write, the Endangered Species Act is under attack. Congress will take the teeth out of it sooner or later, but maybe not soon enough to save thousands of working families in the Pacific Northwest. The failed social experiments of this century were based on the idealistic and erroneous assumption that man would willingly relinquish his self-interest for the common good. Lofty pleas for environmental restraint based on similar notions will meet a similar fate.

We fly fishers are no less a narrow interest group than are the timber companies. They know that private ownership is their best course. They already own three-quarters of the land in my county and are acquiring more every day. I am convinced that our interests are also best served through the acquisition of as much private water as possible before it's too late—not only individually, but through our existing groups and organizations and special entities formed for the purpose. We have the talent and resources within our ranks to do this, and all the data indicate that we should do it. If you think we have lost a lot of trout water in the last fifty years, just wait. You ain't seen nothin' yet!

While coastal development, industrial growth, oil spills, and Japanese drift nets are devastating saltwater sport-fishing, the warm-water fisheries are still in pretty good shape. Sunfishes are hardier and more adaptable to changing environmental conditions than are the trouts and, of course, there are a lot more farm ponds in America than trout streams. A bluegill can't live in a toxic waste dump, but he can survive under pretty tough conditions and has shown some tolerance for moderate levels of pollution and acidity. As long as there's a little dissolved oxygen for him to breathe and a bit of something to eat, he can make it in any body of water with a temperature that reaches into the seventies in the summer. I know golf course water hazards that support bluegills despite massive applications of toxic chemicals to nearby lawns, and I can show you some small bluegills in a swampy area below a landfill. Those fish are subjected to the most toxic carcinogens known to man, yet they still cling to life and even reproduce. I know that you would prefer to fish for wild rainbows in a pristine stream than for radioactive bluegills in a garbage dump! Hopefully, landfill angling is a ways down the road yet, but the point is that we will likely have warm waters to fish long after the pristine stream is only a nostalgic memory of a more innocent time.

I take no pleasure in making such harsh remarks and wish I could present a sanguine view of the future. It is apparent to all cognizant observers that really meaningful environmental reform carries an outrageous price tag. Neither the general public nor their elected representatives are going to consider measures that would cost thousands of jobs and destroy entire industries, not to mention asking people to revert to a nineteenth-century lifestyle and overcome their biological and cultural desire to bear offspring. The sociopolitical ramifications of such an agenda are obviously impossible. While sorting trash for the recycling center may make us feel good, such niceties will have little effect on the ultimate outcome. The engine that drives Western Civilization runs only on hard cash. Serious reform is unlikely until, as *Newsweek* said, people actually step in it. By then, of course, it will be too late.

Acidification, siltation, de-oxygenation, and excessive chemical nitrogen present real threats to even the hardy sunfishes. Nonetheless, private lakes and ponds, although dependent on "outside" water sources, can be managed as a closed ecosystem and the water chemistry adjusted as necessary. Although this sort of thing is something less than idyllic, the alternative is no fly fishing at all. Centrarchids are better suited to this kind of managed situation than are the delicate salmonoids (with their comparatively narrow habitat requirements) and don't succumb as easily to attempts at domestication.

Many birds, insects, rodents, and other creatures have adjusted to human activity without becoming domesticated. Some, like rats and cockroaches, occupy ecological niches in the very shadow of man without relinquishing their wild characteristics; others—coons, possums, coyotes—have not only survived but prospered from human habitations. The common house cat is still essentially a wild animal after several millennia of pampering and breeding.

Bass and other sunfishes are higher on the evolutionary ladder than are trouts (don't get upset; spiny-rayed, scaly fishes are generally considered more evolved that soft-rayed fishes) and instinctively recognize man as a dangerous predator. But they are still willing, like squirrels and English sparrows, to occupy the habitat that he wittingly or unwittingly provides. These intelligent fishes will never come flocking to a benefactor the way hatchery trout do at feeding time. They will eat your food and live in your pond, but they will never be your friend!

BIBLIOGRAPHY

Baker, Doug. 1980. *River Place*. Forest Grove, OR: Timber Press.

Borger, Gary A. 1979. *Nymphing*. Harrisburg, PA: Stackpole Books.

———. 1980. *Naturals*. Harrisburg, PA: Stackpole Books.

———. 1991. *Designing Trout Flies*. Wausau, WI: Tomorrow River Press, 1991.

Borror, Donald J., Dwight M. DeLong and Charles A. Triplehorn. 1981. *An Introduction to the Study of Insects*. New York: Saunders College Publishing.

Borror, Donald J., and Richard E. White. 1970. *A Field Guide to the Insects of America North of Mexico*. Boston: Houghton Mifflin.

Conant, Roger. 1975. *A Field Guide to the Reptiles and Amphibians of Eastern and Central North America*. Boston: Houghton Mifflin.

Gasque, Jim. 1946. *Bass Fishing*. New York: Alfred A. Knopf.

Hannah, John Tweed. 1990. *Creative Fishing*. Houston: RFM Publishers.

Hellekson, Terry. 1979. *Popular Fly Patterns*. Salt Lake City: Peregrine Smith.

Henshall, James A. 1881. *Book of the Black Bass*. Cincinnati: Robert Clarke and Co.

Keith, Tom. 1989. *Fly Tying and Fishing for Panfish and Bass*. Portland, OR: Frank Amato Publications.

Knight, John Alden. 1949. *Black Bass*. New York: G.P. Putnam's Sons.

Leonard, J. Edson. 1976. *Essential Fly Tier*. Engelwood Cliffs, NJ: Prentice Hall.

Malo, John. 1981. *Fly Fishing for Panfish*. Minneapolis: Dillon Press.

Mathews, Craig and John Juracek. 1987. *Fly Patterns of Yellowstone*. New York: Lyons & Burford.

McClane, A.J. 1974. *Field Guide to the Freshwater Fishes of North America*. New York: Holt, Rhinehart and Winston.

Milne, Lorus and Margery. 1980. *Audubon Society Field Guide to North American Insects and Spiders*. New York: Alfred A. Knopf.

Meyer, Deke. 1989. *Float Tube Fly Fishing*. Portland, OR: Frank Amato Publications.

Nixon, Tom. 1968. *Fly Tying and Fly Fishing for Bass and Panfish*. New York: A.S. Barnes.

Rosborough, E.H. "Polly." 1988. *Tying and Fishing the Fuzzy Nymphs*, 4th ed. Harrisburg, PA: Stackpole Books.

Schweibert, Ernest. 1955. *Matching the Hatch*. New York: Macmillan Publishing.

Sternberg, Dick. 1987. *Freshwater Gamefish of North America*. Minnetonka, MN: Cy DeCosse Inc.

———— and Bill Ignizio. 1987. *Panfish*. Minnetonka, MN: Cy DeCosse Inc.

Stewart, Dick. 1989. *Bass Flies*. Intervale, NH: Northland Press.

————. 1979. *Universal Fly Tying Guide*. Woodstock, VT: Countryman Press.

———— and Farrow Allen. 1992. *Flies for Bass & Panfish*. Intervale, NH: Northland Press.

Talleur, Dick. 1990. *Versatile Fly Tyer*. New York: Lyons & Burford.

Taylor, Rick. 1979. *Guide to Successful Bass Fishing*. Missoula, MT: Mountain Press.

Tinsley, Russel. 1975. *Panfishing in Texas*. Houston: Cordovan Corp.

Tryon, Chuck and Sharon. 1990. *Figuring Out Flies*. Rolla, MO: Ozark Mountain Flyfishers.

Waterman, Charles. 1989. *Fly Rodding for Bass*. New York: Lyons & Burford.

Whitlock, Dave. 1988. *L.L. Bean Fly Fishing for Bass Handbook*. New York: Lyons & Burford.

————. 1982. *Dave Whitlock's Guide to Aquatic Trout Foods*. New York: Lyons & Burford.

Vines, Robert A. 1977. *Trees of East Texas*. Austin: University of Texas Press.

INDEX